GETTING ALONG

A Guide for Teenagers

Charles S. Mueller

GETTING ALONG

**How to live with yourself,
God, parents, family,
and friends**

AUGSBURG Publishing House • Minneapolis

To Sarah, Chuck, Amy, and Julie
who showed their mother and me
how great Christian teenagers can be

CONTENTS

How This Book
Came into Existence

For more than 10 years I have been accepting invitations to speak to large gatherings of youth in locations from coast to coast and border to border. From such experiences of sharing, I was led to write a book about teenagers and the teenage self-image entitled, *Thank God I'm a Teenager* (Augsburg, 1976). I was helped in that writing task by Dr. Donald Bardill, an outstanding counselor of youth now teaching at Florida State University in Tallahassee. That book contained an offer to answer questions from readers. Hundreds of teenagers took us up on that offer! Some of the material in this book is my response to those questions.

While the letters were pouring in, I continued speaking to more youth groups under the sponsorship of a number of different organizations. I also spoke at congregational gatherings and before large church-wide youth events. In the presentations, I generally asked those present to share their concerns and give witness of their lives. They did. They wrote me notes—all kinds of notes on all kinds of paper. The notes included questions, comments, and observations on a broad range of subjects. I asked them to note their ages and whether they were male or female. Most did. A few of the cities where we gathered, and to which young people came from miles around, were Seattle, Charlotte, Miami, Jefferson City, Chicago, San Antonio, Kansas City, New Orleans, Baltimore, Buffalo, Wichita, Cleveland, Los Angeles, Sacramento, and Minneapolis. And there were other places.

After collecting thousands of notes, I organized them by content. In this process, I discovered that all the concerns were common to every age, to both sexes, and to all geographic locations. Some of the young people had a specific concern a little earlier than others. Some concerns were slightly more common to one sex than the other. Some communities seemed to have a slightly larger number of specific needs than was apparent in another place. But that's about all the difference I noted between regions or ages or sexes.

I began reading the questions of my teenage friends, and making comments, before youth gatherings. I could soon predict the audience response in terms of both intensity and reaction time. The audience authenticated the material in a way that amazed me. I'm convinced that what I'm sharing here is common to Christian kids across the country. As you read this book, have a pen in hand. Underline things. Note the similarity to your own feelings. Some of the phrases will almost haunt you and come back again and again.

Keep in mind that these young people have *not* dropped out of society. They have *not* given up on church or family. While, in the minds of adults, they may be questioning some very sacred things, their queries are actually the kinds of questions kids should have the right to ask as they look for answers. Most of them want to see some changes. All of those who wrote a note or made a comment did so voluntarily—that means they really wanted to say something. I'm glad I can carry their comments to a larger audience.

On the following pages, three things will happen:
1) Teenagers will be allowed to speak for themselves,
2) I will make comments on some of the letters and sharings I have received over the last 10 years,
3) I will constantly point toward the directings in God's Word, which still stands as a "lamp to guide me and light for my path" (Ps. 119:105).

I ask you who read these pages to do four things:
1) Pray,
2) Agree to seek help for your problems,

3) Talk to the people with whom you need to get along (I really mean *talk)* and stand your ground on the need for all of you to share with one another,
4) Consult and share with a pastor (preferably your own) about important questions and concerns.

I believe this book can be a valuable aid to growing because much of its content has been shared with me by excellent youth leaders and splendid men and women of God over the years. My list of teachers includes people like Ed Birner, Leo Symmank, Roland Seboldt, Cliff Pederson, Dave Anderson, Larry Johnson, Jim Woodruff, Kevin Murphy, John Rondema, Fred Kemper, Joel and Becky Sunde, and countless other dedicated people who have practiced a ministry to teenagers before my eyes and who have put their belief in kids on the line week in and week out. And I thank one of the oldest teenagers in history, Dr. Martin Poch, who daily invests heavily in the church of today—God's youth.

I also thank Judy White and my wife, Audrey, who typed these words, and who showed their concern for young people by the patient way they accomplished their good work.

Finally, I thank the tens of thousands of young people who carefully listened, who exuberantly responded, who lovingly shared, and who helped me understand some things I would never have known otherwise.

Now it's time to talk about getting along!

ONE

What Makes
Christian Youth Special?

The teenagers I write to and speak with are not average, run-of-the-mill youngsters. I think they are better than that—much better.

My young friends are not necessarily smarter or better looking or more talented or even more moral than others their age. Even if some of them are, those are not the things that set them apart.

What makes them special?

They are practicing, church-going Christians. That doesn't mean they are perfect. It just means they are trying to let their Christian light shine.

Many of them worked hard to scrape together money for a long weekend at a youth gathering in one of many cities in the United States. It's fun being together with a thousand or more other kids, but it costs money. They thought it worthwhile and saw it as money well spent.

There is more. Many of them wrote. Sometimes it was just a scribbly note scratched on a corner of paper. Sometimes it was a carefully written longer letter. But they wrote. In the writing they were taking a chance. They were risking that I might not take them seriously, or I might make fun of them, or I might betray their trust. I'm glad they wrote.

Those kids have the proven ability to capture and express their feelings and needs and spell them out so others can know what's happening within. They recognize personal problems, analyze them, and express their conclusions with clarity.

While I think my friends are unusual, I don't think they are unique among Christian teenagers. You share their abilities, their feelings, their commitment. Check yourself as you move through these pages. Ask: "Have I ever wanted to say *that?* Have I ever been concerned about *that?*" Judging from the applause and laughter and other reactions I get from teenage audiences as I read aloud their notes and questions, I'm convinced their feelings and wants and joys and hurts and yearnings are common to Christian kids everywhere.

Prepare yourself! You may not like what you read. Most of the messages are negative. Very few of these teenagers affirm what's happening in their lives or express appreciation for parental sacrifices. Most are critical of society or family or self. To help you understand this keep three things in mind as you read.

First, all people are better at stating the negative than the positive. Test this yourself. Draw a line down the middle of a piece of paper. On one side, list 10 things wrong with your family. On the other side, list 10 things that are right. Which was easier to pull together? Which has more fire and life? The negative is easier because we've all had more experience tussling with the negative than the positive of life! For every positive thing parents say to a child, they say a dozen or more negative things. Right? We look for flaws. We're conditioned toward finding fault.

Second, much of the positive in life is assumed. Kids assume their parents love them. That confidence makes them bold to be judgmental. They assume that someone is going to take care of them, so they are often cruelly cutting in their comments about the style of that care. They assume that those who taught them morals and positiveness and Christian conduct are practicing these things themselves. They are bold to point out when that's not so.

Third, teenagers are disturbingly truthful and frightfully honest. They tell it like it is! Much of the world *is* negative! Sin *is* rampant in society. Abuse of the human spirit, of the neighbor, of the friend of another color, of the poor takes place publicly all the time. All of these are negatives. Much of the world operates with a different kind of golden rule: Those that have the gold make the rule. That "golden rule" functions in many Christian homes too. Aren't broken rules at home punished by cutting off allowances or removing privileges or some sort of materialistic punishment? Teenage negativism is really nothing more than a reflection of the negative life-style young people see all around them.

One 14-year-old boy wrote, *"Adults don't understand what I can do."* I've never read that sentence to a teenage crowd without getting immediate agreement. But I've never let a teenage crowd off the hook without saying, "And what have you done to help your parents and other adults genuinely know what you can do?" Teenagers must make sure others know of their ability and must demonstrate their potential in their actions.

A 17-year-old girl had this feeling about the future: *"I feel like everything is falling in, I'm never gonna get where I want to be."* That's not surprising. A lot of kids (and adults) feel that way. They're very apprehensive about tomorrow. They don't see people driving less, or being more careful about the use of natural resources, or working harder for a better future for all the world's citizens. They see parents who want to get ahead—no matter what the cost—and who encourage their style of achievement as an unwanted goal upon their sons and daughters. Sons and daughters watch parents carefully and make judgments. Those judgments are often awesomely accurate.

The statement that invariably gets the greatest response was written by a frustrated young man of 15. His sentence has no punctuation, except the first comma, and should be read in one breath. *"Why, when I am having a discussion with my parents they say what they think and then they say I don't want to talk about it anymore."* Read it again. No pause. Without exception, that incredible sentence results in a spasm of laughter and applause —every time. What he's really talking about is incomplete and one-sided communication. Many people who are older don't think young people have anything to say from which they might profit. Teenagers disagree.

My teenage friends spot all kinds of pain in their world. Two young men, one from Seattle and one from Kansas City, wrote these very lucid and touching notes. *"My*

problem is my dad's drinking and drug problem. He is a total pain in the rear, and I don't know quite what to do." Did you notice that he didn't say he was going to abandon, or leave, his father? He wants to *do* something positive. He just doesn't know what! The other one wrote this: "*My dad has told me he doesn't love me and that he just doesn't like being around me. I know I don't love him and really wish I didn't live at home. My mom and I share a mutual love although we have our differences and she's the one that keeps me at home. Living with my dad is torture and I believe it's messing my life up.*" Often confused life standards result for many adults when they slip beyond the teenage years without resolving their own family tensions and try to work them out later under all kinds of twisted philosophies.

Here's a note from a 15-year-old girl: "*Mother and I don't agree on what I should be like. I want to be like I want to be, she wants me to be the way she wants.*" Read it again. Guess who will win? I wonder why parents keep trying to do the impossible? It's not that they shouldn't try to influence or guide their children. But they should know it's not possible to fully control them. And it is absolutely impossible for parents to force their children to do things the parents think are correct without the youngsters' willing participation. It's one thing to try shaping a person's moral character, or intellect, or even to contribute toward someone's spiritual development. But when parent and child disagree on "what I should be like," the exertion of more parental pressure doesn't help.

We still see the problem of the favorite child experienced by Joseph of old (Genesis 37). One boy wrote: "*My mother overloves me, and my brother and my sister see it and hate me. In her opinion, all her kids have turned out basically rotten but me. She sees me as her only chance to say 'That's my son' and be proud of it. My sisters and brothers go as far as degrading me in front of my friends and associates. What is the answer?*" I wondered as I read that whether his 20th century life would develop the same tragic pattern that was played out 3000 years ago in Egypt.

Here's the perception of a 16-year-old written from the backseat of life. Two sentences. What do you think the relationship between the two is? "*I can't talk to my dad* like I used to—a lot of times it seems he doesn't pay attention to what I do. Why does it look like other families have so much fun when they're together and when we are together there seems to be inside gripes and grudges that stop us from having fun?"

I like this note from a 17-year-old Chicago girl. I had to read it twice before I picked up her subtle confession in the last phrase. Check it out against Matt. 7:1-5. She wrote: *"The incidents are too numerous to mention any one case. I fail constantly to deal with my parents as I would with Christ; I lack patience. Part of the problem lies with them. However, I would like to remove the log from my parents' eyes."* What a super last sentence!

Here's a cry for help. *"My family is breaking up. All the kids are falling apart. What do we do?"* Those words from a Seattle 15-year-old sound like the final message from inside a city about to fall to the enemy! Those words are touching, but no less than these words from a young man just past his teenage years: *"I've always loved and still love my family, but it's sure a lot easier to like them since I don't live at home any more."* How many people have discovered *that* to be true! But why?

A young girl from the East wrote, *"I worry too much about people I care for."* Caring is a characteristic of many teenagers. Teenagers are really concerned about brothers and sisters, mothers and fathers, and friends. They care deeply and they worry about them constantly. What a blessing for those of us who are worried over—and prayed for—by teenage "carers." What a burden for those who care so much and yet often feel frustrated in their desire to reach out and help. We need to hear this concern—and teenagers need to share it!

I like this story a young girl wrote. I don't know the details, but I like her perception of the treatment she received and how she responded to it. She began by saying, *"Do you remember the note you read about the girl whose curfew is 12:00 and no later? My curfew is 12:30 Friday and Saturday night. Last summer I went out at 7:30 Saturday and came home at 3:30. Sunday I told my mom and she cared but she didn't make a big deal out of it. But since then I've been home before 12:30 just for my mom and dad. Sometimes I feel that 12:30 is too early for me, but my next-door neighbor is 16, has a driver's* license, and has a curfew of 11:30 so I consider myself lucky."

I regularly get notes which remind me that one of the leading causes for death among teenagers is suicide. I believe many of those suicide deaths are the result of "accidents" in which young people want to do something dramatic but don't calculate the consequences closely enough. They didn't really understand how far they could go with their action before there was no reversal—or didn't realize there might be no one to "stop" them. We must affirm life constantly—it's God's wonderful gift to all of us. We need to speak out for abundant Christian living, especially in the face of words like these: *"What do you do when you feel no one cares about you except God so you try suicide and you always come out of it? I'm just asking for help!"* Whether the 14-year-old who wrote that last note was being overly dramatic, I don't know. But cries for help must be heard first and analyzed later.

Some problems for teenagers are caused by parents who overcompensate for the potential problems of successive children. When one of the children has a difficulty in growing, the parents often assume the next child (and all following children) will inevitably do the same things. Kids resent that. They resent it deeply. One girl wrote, *"My mother and father are always worrying about me, especially Mom. I think it's because I'm the youngest and my older sister got into trouble."* Not all young people follow the pattern of their predecessors—bad or good! Each will walk his or her own path.

This next note is perhaps as explosive as I've ever received. It's a ticking time bomb. When and how will it blow? A 19-year-old shared these words, *"There's really no conflict in my family . . . just no contact. Everyone runs off to different activities and my parents never ask about what I'm doing or anything."*

I'd like to share four longer notes without comment. I found the words touching, full of much caring, often wise. I know them to be universal even though most of us have difficulty admitting it.

One: *"My brother is on drugs. He has left home many times but comes back when he runs out of money. He and my parents are always fighting. They can't understand why I get upset. I love them all, but they are all trying*

18

to pull me and my younger brother to their side of the issue. I feel like I'm being pulled between two elephants. I can't take this much longer. I can't concentrate on anything and my grades are falling. I wish there could be an easy answer. My parents get mad if I try to talk to a friend about it. I can't talk to them so what else can I do? If I try to talk with them they yell at me and I hate fighting."

Two: "My mom and I fought about everything. Thought I hated her. Was sure leaving home was the solution. Never did. Mom went to a mental hospital with a severe disorder, now I wish we'd fight, talk, or anything. I realize how much I love her and need her. I feel guilty now, the things we fought about weren't worth wasting the precious time we had together to share our love for each other. If she gets well, there will be a lot of changes. But we'll never get back the years that we wasted in hatred for each other."

Three: "My father died about six years ago. We never really got along. As a matter of fact I would be punished and sent to my room more times than not. I always wished him dead, and when he died I put the blame all on myself. And for six years I've had a tremendous guilt complex. I came here to find an answer, I don't know how or what kind, but just an answer. I prayed to God but still felt that I was troubled, but when I sat there listening and concentrating on what you were speaking on, I felt a cool chill come over my body. It wasn't the coolness of the room. It was Christ telling me in my heart I was forgiven and I shouldn't feel guilty anymore. I found my answer. And I am at peace with God and myself. Thank you for showing me how to put Christ in my heart."

Four: " I have a small problem. I can't communicate with my dad and he's never around. He died 13 years ago."

Among my favorite real-life commentaries is this plaintive report of a 13-year-old boy. "I don't get along with my mom or sister, my mom especially. She must think our house is a museum, everything I touch, lean on, or sit on, she always hollers at me, I can't even live in my own house. She never changes, not a day goes by she's not hollering at me for something. Practically you have to have new or clean clothes on just to sit down. I can't even *touch anything, or my mom would holler for fooling with it."*

That may strike you as funny—I laughed at first. But it goes deeper. Many young people feel that other members in their families are overwhelmingly and unreasonably committed to cleanliness. There must be some epic struggles about that subject! Never forget—there is *no* Bible passage which says, "Cleanliness is next to godliness." As a matter of fact, when the Lord determined to create people, he began with a mound of dirt (Gen. 2:7). One Buffalo boy became so incensed about his home life that he was persuaded his sister was "clean crazy." How's that for descriptive language! Homes are to be lived in. People who live in them are sometimes not very clean. There are times in their lives when people aren't very tidy either. Pressing a person toward tidiness and cleanliness is not wrong. But there are limits. If the cost is driving all the fun out of life, a clean house isn't worth it!

At one of the youth gatherings I received two notes. One was from a man, 42 years old, and the other from a young lady of 15. When asked to identify their family problems, the man wrote one word: *"Communication."* The next note was from the young lady, who wrote two words, *"No communication."* I wondered when I read the two notes whether they were father and daughter. They certainly could have been. If not, they were certainly someone's father and someone's daughter—both of whom knew their difficulty.

Not all the messages are negative, however. There also are significant numbers of teenage voices that are positive and affirming, especially about their families.

"I won't say I don't have problems but I have a mother, father, and two brothers who will always listen to me, and try to understand and help me." Those great words were written by a 16-year-old girl.

"My parents are so super because they trust me and let me take on my responsibilities without criticizing me. They give advice and I love it and usually accept it. It usually does turn out for the best." Those words were written by a girl, 17.

"I'm a male age 16. At my house, sure my family has its share of arguments and disagreements, but I don't think I could have been half the person I am if it hadn't

been for my parents. My dad just found out that we're going to be transferred to Minnesota. Well, I'm afraid and sad to say the least, but I trust my Mom and Dad enough that I know that they care enough for me and my future that they will take their time and try to help me make it through it. Also I love them enough not to make trouble because I know that it's a great opportunity for my dad. One thing I can say and know it's true for sure, my parents love me and I love them."

"My parents and I have some difficulties but we always manage to work them out. They always listen to my point of view." How's that for a supporting message from an 18-year-old Texas young man?

These last two notes are from a young man and a young lady, one from Missouri and one from Kansas.

"I don't really have a problem communicating with my parents, except I get the feeling they still think of me as a kid. I'm 16 and I've been trusted by them all the time, but it seems like now they give me the impression that I'm going to go wild or something. I wouldn't think of doing that to them for anything in the world. I respect them a whole lot and have always loved them and they love me too. I couldn't hurt them after all they've done for me and the rest of my family. They did without to give to us and they help us whenever we need help. They are really terrific and I don't know what I would do without them. I praise the Lord for giving me such wonderful parents and that they cared enough to bring me into this wonderful and beautiful world."

"I've been brought up in a Christian home and have had the influence of two wonderful parents trying to help me become a whole person. Naturally, there have been hard times, and conflicts have been many. The problem is trying to change from a child into an adult, accept that yourself, and have your parents realize the situation too. Our family is always going in different directions which poses a lot of problems. Our family tends to draw apart because of this but somehow through prayer we come through. I try to keep an open mind but it becomes difficult at times to be patient with parents. God gave them to me and I have been blessed with them. Whatever problems arise, I don't intend to give up. My parents have allowed me to make mistakes and learn and we keep *communication lines open pretty well. I'm beginning to appreciate more and more the humanness and wisdom of my parents."*

There are some great positive things happening in our Christian families! There *are* some unusual young people in our world. There would be a lot more of them if we all worked harder at developing communication and trust. Please note that I said "developing." That's the way it comes to us. Parents and teenagers *develop* their relationships in the areas of communication and trust. It takes time and commitment.

These comments give an indication of how many good, solid, Christian kids think and feel. They also serve as illustrations of some of the troubles these kids face. I am sharing the feelings of some special Christian kids. If this is how it is with them, how must it be with the others? (Luke 23:31).

How did you get along with the observations you read? Were you disturbed? Comfortable? Frustrated? Before you move on recall again the words of our Lord Jesus Christ from John 3, verses 16 and 17: "For God loved the world so much that he gave his only Son, so that everyone who believes in him may not die but have eternal life. For God did not send his Son into the world to be its judge, but to be its savior."

God did not come into the world, in his Son Jesus Christ, so that the world (that includes you) would end up under condemnation, even though the world does deserve that divine response! He came with his judgment and his incisiveness about issues and concerns so that the people might see themselves and their need for a Savior; so they might be led to yearn for the wonder of his grace; so they might be taught to accept the necessity of his mercy; so they might be urged to see the blessing of his forgiveness. Out of that learning each can receive the further promise of the Lord's peace.

An honest look at yourself and your circumstance may at first be somewhat depressing. But look deeper! Be convinced, as I have been convinced so many times, that no situation is beyond his ability to relieve—even though it may be clearly beyond yours. "Humble yourselves, then, under God's mighty hand, so that he will lift you up in his own good time. Leave all your worries with him, because he cares for you" (1 Peter 5:6-7). There is much reason for humility. We fail. Yet the good news in Jesus Christ assures us that he can exalt us in due season. All of us: teenagers, parents, concerned people. Call upon him for his promised help! He will hear—and answer!

TWO

Getting Along
with Yourself

There are a lot of young people who dislike themselves. I know. I meet them all the time. When asked, "What's your biggest problem?" a Charlotte, North Carolina, 16-year-old simply said, "*Me.*" A 14-year-old boy from Chicago was a little more descriptive: "*My mom and dad are always giving me a chance to communicate during arguments but I don't know how to express myself.*" A Jefferson City young man put it this way, "*I can't understand me.*" A San Jose girl analyzed her problems saying: "*I can't find anyone to love or to love me physically and spiritually. Could it be because I don't love myself?*"

Sometimes they laugh about their self-images, but it's gallows humor. A 16-year-old put his negative self-analysis in these words: "*Why do mothers say be yourself, but hate it when you are?*"

Teenagers can be brutally analytical and frank about themselves, like this young lady from San Antonio: "*Isn't it true that sometimes when someone hurts you instead of trying to get over it, you cry and feel sorry for yourself —and sort of like being hurt?*"

The most common response to a request asking teenagers to pinpoint their biggest problem is the answer, "I am." When young people start talking about this subject and get comfortable in the conversation (that means they don't feel threatened or on trial), they generally take

24

full responsibility for their difficulties. They recognize and accept their part in developing the unhappy circumstances of their lives. They realize they often do irrational and negative things—and do them to people for whom they deeply care—for no apparent reason! They even realize that one of the characteristics of the teenage years is poor judgment, usually the result of limited experience.

How can you learn to like yourself? I'd like to suggest ways for improving your self-image. Then it's up to you. Ready? Let's go!

Improving our self-image is a crucial necessity for most of us. A poor self-image, extended across a lifetime, brings years of unhappiness. This unhappiness first comes to the person who has a bad image of himself or herself. Then it leaks out and stains almost everyone that person touches. Erik Erikson, a well-known counselor, believes that one of the first tasks of life is learning to trust yourself. That includes developing a proper loving appreciation for who you are.

We all want to accept ourselves. The yearning to develop self-confidence starts from the time toddlers take their first steps. It stretches on until life's final days. Jesus said building self-respect is important—it is the basis for loving others. Remember his encouragement to "love your neighbor as you love yourself" (Luke 10:27). If you don't love yourself, how can you love your neighbor? A proper respect for who you are, and developing the process for achieving that respect, is one of life's important early tasks. People who have trouble living comfortably with others generally have difficulty living comfortably with themselves.

You and your self-image

There's a difference between having a bad self-image that can be changed and having a clear perception of a personal problem that can't. One 16-year-old determined his basic problem in life in one word: *acne*. He didn't have a warped self-image. He had zits! *They* needed attention—medical or cosmetic treatment! That was his primary problem, not his self-image. When a New Mexico boy wrote me, *"How does a fat boy get a date?"*, he was well on his way toward solving his own problem by hon-

estly facing his personal condition. He was fat. Fat boys don't get many dates. But ex-fat boys do OK.

A young man of 18 left me this note: *"I enjoy life very much. My only real problem is I'm an epileptic. But I don't let it get me down. I'm a teenager and I think this is probably the best time in my life. I enjoy things just as much as everyone else."* He's confronted his problem head-on. A 16-year-old girl was just as sharp in self-analysis. Her comment read: *"My parents realize I'm a daydreamer and they feel this affects my responsibility, which it does."* She knew her parents were right and she accepted both their judgment and the effects of her own actions.

To my mind there is a great difference between these examples of genuine personal problems (all of which have some kind of physical or psychological aspect to them) and dealing with a poor self-image. Poor self-images sound more like this: "I'm a sad and very depressed person. I don't like myself." "I don't like my attitude toward myself." "I can't feel good about me." Why do teenagers feel that way about themselves?

While there are a lot of possible reasons, high on my own list is this one: Many teenagers don't understand themselves. A lot of teenagers grow up without a clear picture of their possibilities in life; without a clear understanding of what's happening all around them; without a clear recognition of the legitimate goals of life. If these things are out of focus, they are sure to have trouble "seeing" themselves and their situation. What they need are some "superlenses" for studying themselves. I'm happy to report that at least three such lenses exist and are available for use by all!

The first "lens" is the Bible. Not only does it contain the message of salvation in Jesus Christ (that's its primary and most important theme), but it also has some clear-eyed catalogs of goals for human conduct and many suggestions for legitimate styles of living. The Bible is a great book for teenagers!

For a second "lens," get your hands on some of the many books that present a readable description of what the teenage years are and can be like. You might want to read a book I wrote with Dr. Donald Bardill entitled

Thank God I'm a Teenager (Augsburg, 1976). Thousands of young people have found it useful.

As a third "lens," pick out an experienced adult counselor with whom you can talk. I usually suggest pastors (maybe it's because I am one) or school counselors (because I've seen and met some super ones) or a trusted relative (an uncle, a cousin, a grandfather). Talk with them! Any of them. All of them.

I'm not suggesting that you should ignore your parents as persons who can help you see life clearly. But often a more detached opinion seems to offer better and quicker help. Using those three suggested "lenses" will help develop confidence in the ability of another surefire helper —*you.*

An 18-year-old from Charlotte, North Carolina, discovered his *you.* He wrote, *"Most people really don't know me—the real me."* He sounds like he'd like to have people meet his "real me." That doesn't mean he's perfect, or thinks he's perfect, or believes he's a very super person. Not at all. He just wants you to know what he's really like.

Is this the place to say you're going to have to recognize that change will take place in you? Change isn't an enemy. It's an inevitable and necessary friend. As you grow physically, emotionally, and spiritually, you will change. That's OK. Just think of the changes you have already undergone in life! If you hadn't changed, you'd still be who you were five or ten years ago. Look what you'd have missed!

Change is necessary. The normal pattern of life as we grow older is to make moves from *dependence* (in the extreme condition of dependence, you were lying on someone's lap with a bottle stuck in your mouth!) to *interdependence* (in that phase, you learned to do things for parents or brothers and sisters or friends, but got things done for yourself in return) toward *independence* (you never get there, but it's an interesting goal). Your teenage years are largely spent working out that three-step sequence on the various levels of your life. Examples? Sure!

"My mother and I disagree on my responsibility. My mother doesn't let me do anything. She's afraid to let me go."

"Both my parents work and I'm the eldest so I am responsible for keeping up the household. I'd like a chance to do what I want, not always what they want me to do."

"I'm an 18-year-old girl. I'm tired of living at home. I know that's terrible but I've been so good to my family and always helping. I need to be alone and away from my family. Unfortunately, my mom doesn't accept this. Things will change next year when I'm off to college. I'm sure I'll miss them terribly."

There's nothing wrong with the feelings of those three teenagers! They all are expressions of moving from one level of relationship to another. *How* that changing takes place may vary from one situation to another. *That* it will take place is inevitable.

Let me offer an important word of caution. There are unacceptable ways of changing. Sometimes you yearn for recognition from others so much that you're willing to do things that are morally wrong or physically dangerous or just plain dumb. Most of you know when that's what is happening. If you're not sure, check out those three "lenses" for seeing yourself we mentioned a couple of paragraphs back. You'll soon know what's right.

While changing is all right, not every change is necessarily the best thing for you. For those times when you are uncomfortable about a decision to change, I will pass on some advice Pastor William Bruening used to give. He'd say: "When in doubt—don't." That's good advice. The right way to go is generally quite clear. You'll soon see an obvious path develop through a haze of confusion. If it takes a while to appear, don't worry. Just work at it, wait, and an answer will come.

I really was struck with this note from a girl in Wichita, Kansas. *"I feel good. I feel happy about my life. I wonder about some things, though. I'm not sure if I'm overlooking something that could be better. I don't think I'm as sensitive as I could be. Dad and I have a good relationship. But he's a quiet guy and I never know his opinions, even if I ask him. When he's hurt, he clams up. I hope they trust me, because they are the ones who have made me the person I am now."* That's really a super self-view. You can have one just like it. Read on!

Your self-image and your parents

If claiming responsibility for their own personal difficulties is the most common reaction of teenagers to their circumstances, pointing to their parents as the reason for their problems comes in a close second. Many teenagers feel their parents don't give them the room they need to grow. They are pretty sharp in their analysis of the problem. Listen to this bright young lady: *"My father can't or won't accept the fact that I'm not the little girl he knew. My mother has accepted it, and treats me in a way that I feel like a person, not a baby. My father thinks I have no sense, he's told me so often I really begin to have doubts about myself."*

Moms don't escape judgment. They get their share of attention as well. *"I feel my mom is too overprotective. She won't let me make my own decisions. It's either her way or not at all. What shall I do?"* The writer of that note has done one important thing already—she has analyzed her problem and come to a conclusion!

Teenagers recognize a conflict in parental advice. Two boys, one 16 and one 17, from Minneapolis, described their circumstances: *"They say they want me to be independent and learn to do things for myself but they don't want to let me go out on my own. They don't even want me to get my own job,"* and *"My parents find it hard to accept me for what I am."* An 18-year-old daughter put it this way: *"My parents don't accept me as an adult because I'm still at home."*

When parents get too involved with the decision making of a young person, the results don't turn out well—for anybody. One young person wrote: *"I'm afraid of getting older and leaving home."* I wonder who built that feeling? And sometimes the parents get surprised: *"My parents get upset because I don't always share my problems or thoughts with them. I like to work through my problems on my own and my parents can't understand my not wanting to talk about them until I have things figured out. I don't confide in people often. They haven't wanted to talk or share until the last year or so and they expect to be my best friend just like that."* Isn't that something? What a superb insight! Nothing wrong with *that* teenager's analytical abilities!

Of course, these are just general observations which may or may not speak to the circumstance you face. Let me share a few specific concerns affecting teenagers and their parents as illustrations of how the development of a positive self-image can be hindered.

One thing that triggers a teenage reaction and frustrates maturing is *parental hovering.* Sometimes parents get so close kids don't have room for necessary independent decision making. When parents stand too close, they can't see what's happening right before their eyes! Listen to this: *"My mom doesn't trust me to manage my money. I'm the treasurer of our youth group."* Did you hear? He said that his friends trust him with *their* money, but his own mother won't show the same confidence with *his own* money!

Same message, different words from a young lady, 15: *"I get very mad and crabby at my mom for no reason at all and she sure doesn't make it any better. My mom and dad want me to wear dresses a lot of time like almost every day to school."* I wonder how old that young lady will have to be before she has a chance to decide what she should wear?

And rooms! How many notes I get about rooms! I don't know what this guy's room looks like: *"My last conflict was with my mother—a year ago she said I could keep my room the way I wanted it and she still bothers me about it."* What's really bugging him is the fact that a deal was made and his mother won't keep her bargain! She's hovering!

I got a laugh from a 15-year-old boy's question, *"My family isn't too sure whether I should be a bartender. Bartending isn't sinful, right?"* I don't know whether bartending, sinful or not, is a vocation you adopt at 15. But if that young man has smart parents, they will realize that whatever he is going to be in life will finally be *his* decision. They will want to influence, but not try to direct, his actions. Directing doesn't work. Or rather, I should say, directing doesn't work well. If parents push long enough, they may get their way, but they'll also have a very angry or depressed or frustrated son or daughter on their hands for years to come.

Young people need room to live. You need a chance to make your own decisions. You need to learn to control

31

yourselves. One of the greatest definitions of maturity I've ever heard is: "Maturity is the disciplined obedience to the unenforceable." Why don't you read that again? It means you can't "make" people do the right thing. If anyone is going to make someone do the right thing, it has to be that person himself. When mothers and fathers hover over their sons and daughters, fussing about haircuts and room care and eating and all kinds of other strange things which ought to be in the realm of teenage decision making, there's trouble afoot. That doesn't mean parents shouldn't tell their children what's right. But once they've made their point, they should let life's process take over. Some things are learned best when learned alone.

And what about your responsibility toward your parents' advice? It's a stupid son who immediately takes the opposite position to everything his father says! You are responsible for building your own record of personal dependability and competence with your parents, so that mom and dad can *know* if they've done their part! For example, I wonder if that 17-year-old treasurer had told his mom about his position? You teenagers owe your parents clear messages about things like that.

If hovering over teenagers gets them upset, *comparing them with others* makes them furious. They don't like it. *"How can I get my parents to stop comparing me with my brothers and sisters?" "My mom and dad don't get along with my sister and they are always telling me not to grow up like her and that makes me feel bad because I love her very much." "My brother and sister have always done things my parents don't approve of, so they always think I will do something they won't approve of."*

Teenagers don't like comparisons that downgrade them or other people they love. Parents certainly have a responsibility to warn and admonish their sons and daughters. Sometimes they may have to make a comparison to make a point. But that technique wears out very quickly. When overused, comparisons make people feel dumb or inadequate or trapped within a spiral of inevitability.

What can you do when people start comparing you to others? Claim your own individuality! Let it be known that you are a you. Be as low-key as you can in the process, however. No matter how provoked you get, you must recognize that the world doesn't need another stamping, shouting, crying teenager! But be emphatic—especially with yourself. Say to yourself: "I'm a unique individual whom God has made and I will rejoice and be glad." It's true. Then tell your folks—*clearly!*

The number three problem on the list is *parental nosiness* or *prying* or *snooping*. The specifics range over a wide area. One young person wanted to know, *"whether or not it's OK if a parent reads something personal and uses it against you."* Another plainly stated, *"I don't like parents being snoopy."* A Minneapolis youngster said it this way: *"They always are wanting to know what you are doing where you are doing it and who you are doing it with . . . they always seem to worry too much, they are always asking questions, prying into me."* And the crushing comment from a young girl about her mother, *"She's always invading my privacy and says she really wants to know and help, but we're not that close."*

This is a very sensitive subject. Of course parents have a right and responsibility to know a great deal about what teenagers are doing and where they are going. Parents are morally and legally liable. But moms and dads really ought to be careful how they exercise that responsibility! Reading another's mail, going through drawers in a room, and intensive interrogation are all steps that should be taken with the greatest reluctance and then only in the face of the most serious provocation.

This subject of teenage privacy is definitely a subject needing discussion. As a teenager, you have a distinct responsibility in this area too. There *is* such a thing as being excessively secretive and indefensibly reserved. Parents have a right to show care for their children by making appropriate inquiries. Children have a responsibility to share with their folks. A young lady from Texas expressed an extreme and wrong-headed teenage reaction when she wrote: *"My mom and I get in lots of fights because I'm superindependent. After being at school all day, being polite and nice, I like to go upstairs to my room and be myself. Get away from everyone. She wants me down with the family and I just can't."* Superindependent! She said it herself. Being asked to spend reasonable amounts of time with parents and other family members is not an invasion of your privacy! It sounds to me like she has a double standard. She's pleasant to others and pouty at home. That's not fair to the people who have a proven record of surrounding you with love and care.

But there's another side stated by a girl from Minneapolis, 18, when she complained about her parents: *"They don't respect me for my opinions. I don't like to talk about my life or anything to my parents because they don't seem to understand what I mean, twisting and changing to suit what they want or expect to hear, usually making a situation worse than what it is."*

We all grow up. It's difficult to grow up at home where there is great pressure (generally unintentional) to keep us children. Parents are inclined to hover and compare and pry. They ought to recognize that inclination and make a determined effort toward resisting those extremes. You need breathing room. You need a chance to be who you are. You have a right to considerable privacy. But all those rights are better protected, and abuses better restrained, through open discussion. Both parents and teenagers need to work hard at that open discussion. You really haven't developed a positive self-image until you've learned how to talk with your family about the issues that are most important to your life. No one can give you a positive self-image on a silver platter. This is also true: No one can take it from you against your will. If you want others to recognize your uniqueness, recognize it yourself first. If you want others to prize who you are, prize yourself first. You can and ought to be gentle and firm and caring as you claim your personal life, but also accept your responsibilities for family living. Help your parents help you.

Your self-image and your friends

Getting comfortable with yourself and learning how to get along with your family isn't all there is to life! There's a lot more world out there! There are millions and millions of people who don't belong to your family but who are still very important to you and the way you live. With some of those people you will want to develop a special kind of close relationship which is called friendship. Everyone needs some friends. God said that it's not good to be alone (Gen. 2:18) and a 13-year-old boy from Virginia agreed when he wrote, *"I feel that Im left out because I have two sisters and they're both older and I don't have any friends."* Just in case you think he's a one-in-a-million teenager, here are more: *"My biggest problem is I don't fit in. I can't find anyone to listen to me or take me seriously." "The thing most disturbing to me? Not being liked by people." "How can I make friends easily?" "The thing that is disturbing my life most is getting along with other people." "Sometimes—no, a lot of times I think people really don't like me but tolerate me. I isolate myself by saying they isolate me. What can I do?"* Enough examples to make the point? There are more!

Having friends is important. Developing the ability to gain and keep friends is critical in life. Like many other abilities, the basic skills of friending are related to your self-image! If you have a bad self-image, you'll have trouble doing friendly things. As an example, just look at one of the earliest methods of developing friendships with members of the opposite sex—dancing. For a lot of teenagers, asking someone to dance seems to be the toughest task they ever face. I am consistently asked the question, "How do you ask a girl (or guy) to dance?" That question comes from every section of the country. The answer is simple. You walk right up to someone at a dance, give a little smile, and pleasantly ask, "Want to dance?" That's it. That's all there is to it. So what's the big deal?

The big deal is that the guy is scared the girl is going to say no. He's afraid she's going to reject him—and do it in such a way that he'll feel embarrassed or degraded. That's *his* "big deal." A girl often will not go to a dance for fear that no one will ask her to dance. That's *her* "big deal." Not being asked to dance is just as embarrassing and degrading as being refused. The truth of the matter is that friendly people get danced with most of the time. The world isn't out there waiting to reject you or say no to you. Much of the world is out there wanting to say yes.

Finding out whether that last statement is true for you is one of the great risks of life. I won't kid you—life has its risks. Those risks are more easily accepted if you have a healthy respect for yourself and can communicate that understanding of self to others. Just look around. Is it really the prettiest girl who gets most of the requests to dance? Does the handsomest guy dance the most? Isn't it actually the ones who are relaxed, self-assured, and friendly who fit both those desirable categories? I refer to the ones who handle themselves in a way that shows they have self-respect and who show they can take chances meeting new people in new situations—aren't they the ones that get the breaks? In order to have friends, you need to be friendly toward yourself first.

Yet a caution is in order. Sometimes we decide to sell out and strive to gain friends in what looks like an easier way—by compromising ourselves. That's the opposite of self-respect. Listen to a girl talk about herself: *"I can't be me around other people. I always change to be accepted. Sometimes I just get so frustrated about it I break up and cry. I try being myself, but I know my friends wouldn't like me any better if I was myself. I know I should be myself, but it's too hard feeling rejection."*

Now hear the observations of two other keen-eyed teen-agers: *"Help! My brother has a real poor self-image. He goes around saying no one likes me and I hate myself (he's really weird) and other things that drive me crazy. He only has a few friends and they're all weird too. He never goes out."* *"There's a girl in our school who seems to have an insecure place in her life. She seems to want to lie and outdo others. What can I do to help?"*

I have a feeling that the girl in the school who does those things is the girl who wrote the note. The answer to her question? Don't do things to yourself that will hurt you. Respect and love who you are. The lying has to go, and the "outdoing" as well.

One way to confront those negative feelings about yourself is with a question that a Seattle girl asked: *"Should I try to be what other people want me to be (looks, action) or be what I want to be myself?"*

Sooner or later everyone has to answer that question. The sooner each of us decides to be what we can and want to be and what we know to be correct, and do it in a way that recognizes that it is all part of God's will for us, the better off we'll be. Ask God to help you develop a powerful self-acceptance. Pray for wisdom to know what, in terms of self-acceptance, you should do.

But where do we begin? What's a good place to start claiming responsibility for ourselves?

A lovely young lady from Alhambra, California, shared something in a group I was with that will help you know where to begin. The young people at Alhambra were talking about what to do when the group they're with wants to do something they feel is not too smart—or even wrong. They wanted to know what they could say so their words wouldn't sound pious or judgmental or preachy. She told them that she had a magic sentence which she used whenever she was asked to do something she didn't feel right about. That magic sentence helped her stand up straight, didn't attack the group, made her point, and gave everyone a chance to change with dignity. When asked her magic sentence, this is what she said: "I'm sorry I can't do that. It wouldn't be right for me."

What a great response that is! It states her position. It doesn't destroy further conversation with friends. It claims personal responsibility.

Try it out. See if it doesn't work! You won't lose self-respect or friends or anything else (except fear) with that sentence. You'll gain, and you'll find you help others when you talk that way. And what's friendlier than helping a friend? What a great way to build your self-image and self-respect!

Have you ever wondered why God gave us so many years to grow up? It takes 20 years for the world to suggest that you may finally be an adult. Why does it take so long?

One possible reason is we need that much time to make the many, many learning mistakes that are part of life. It's not possible to grow up without making mistakes. But one of the great lessons of the growing years is learning from mistakes—how to correct them; how to understand them; how to accept ourselves when we make them. We aren't perfect. That's another way of saying that we sin. We fail. We stumble. We act like people.

God knows that. That's why his plan, established before the beginning of history (Ephesians 1), was directly related to our making mistakes. In the cross of Christ, God offers forgiveness for the mistakes we make, and by the power of the Holy Spirit, he gives us the capacity to accept forgiveness and to change. Not only are we given the capacity to change, but God himself in his Word and through his will becomes our teacher, leading us. You are his. He called you into being and claimed you in creation. He reclaimed you in redemption. He makes you his through his sanctifying power. You are his. Use that short sentence as the cornerstone of your self-respect. You are his. He loves you. He wants you. He accepts you. Build on that. If God feels that way toward you, how dare you feel any different toward yourself? If he says you are something special and has proven it with his care, you must be!

Start getting your life together around that focal point! Begin with God's understanding and acceptance of you and then review your understanding of yourself. Respect what you are in him. Start throwing away those things in your life that aren't usable for him—or helpful for yourself. Love those things in yourself that he loves. Claim those things in yourself that he claims. Respect those things in yourself that he respects. Finally, accept what he accepts: *you.*

Then look out! A whole new era of experience is building! New worlds are opening! Life will get better and better. It will happen to you and for you. Trust in him. Call upon him in need. Hear his Word and seek his will for your life, and let the Spirit guide you to follow. You'll soon develop the basic skills necessary for getting along with yourself, and will then be ready to reach out successfully to others!

THREE

Getting Along
with Your Parents

Most of the notes and letters I get from teenagers have
to do with their homes and families. A lot of their concerns have to do with parents.

There have been some great homes and great families
in our world—there still are. There have been some great
parents in history—there still are. Some people feel positive about the past by remembering the way it was in
their home as they grew. Others observe the positive
things in the homes and families that surround them now.
The sad part of it is that most of us reach positive conclusions about home too late—long after everyone is grown
and gone and that phase of our lives is finished. Our
negative feelings surface the same way—too late to change
them. That's sad. It's sad because when time and distance
separate us from the family in which we grew up, we
can't do anything to change any parts of that past. We
can't go back and rebuild memories. We can't react later
to an old issue in the new and better way we have
learned. It's too late to change yesterday.

But Christians can change today! That's one reason we
need to talk about our homes and families *now*—so we
can change things as needed. Christians are specialists in
the changing business. We have been changed by God.
We believe God can and does change others. We know
he allows us to be his servants for changing many things

—people included. Here's a message of encouragement for those who want to change their relationship with their parents but are afraid it can't be done. It came from a 15-year-old Cleveland girl. She said: *"For those kids who don't have a good relationship with their parents—try to relate to them. Go to their level because when you are on the same level and get along it's beautiful and like nothing you'll ever experience again."*

What are some general family concerns in our time? Let me list a few.

1. *"My parents won't let me live my life the way I want to."*
2. *"My problem is I can't obey my parents when I think they're wrong."*
3. *"How do you get parents to accept you as you are and not what they wish you were?"*
4. *"Parents don't forget your past. Mom hassles me about getting drunk and taking pills and it was over two years ago. I ran away once, I won't do it again. She holds that against me too. All in the name of love."*
5. *"I have a feeling I want to grow up, but my mother and father try to stifle me."*

Some problem areas visible in those notes are things like independence, personal judgment, parental expectation, parental acceptance, forgiveness, and freedom. Do you see more? Those are all key concerns.

Here are two additional observations that are just as common. *"My parents aren't perfect and I expect them to be. I get very frustrated with myself because of it. How can I accept the fact that they're human?"* And, *"I think that my problem is I really don't want to talk with my parents. I love my mom, but I'm not sure about my dad. I can't wait till I can be on my own."*

Those young people are making some important statements. They recognize that parents aren't perfect. They understand that relating to parents is *their* problem. They acknowledge they are just as likely to be judgmental and quick on the trigger as their parents. Remember: We have the power of God to change. We ourselves, in many instances, are among the things that can and ought to be changed. Pray for God to change your parents, but also pray for God to change you. We all must leave ourselves open to that power of God which builds correctives into the way we act.

I'm not going to push at you with the commandment that orders you to honor your father and mother. That's the law. It's a true command of God, but not a very good base from which to talk about difficulties between parents and teens. Rather, I'd like to begin by listing some of the things that upset teenagers and make it hard for them to honor anybody.

Fathers—God bless them

What's wrong with dads? A boy from Jefferson City said, *"I have an overprotective father."* And a girl from St. Louis wrote, *"In dating, ma trusts me, dad doesn't when a guy drops me off after a date. Dad watches out a window."*

I don't know the precise point of division between being overprotective and being underconcerned. Its location probably has a lot to do with the age of all involved. Before you get upset about overprotective fathers, you ought to check out your father's overall love level, his general attitude of caring, and the way he shows concern for other members of your family. Talk to him. Let him know what things bother you. Be calm. Be reasonable. Speak clearly. Listen carefully to his responses. *Then* determine whether he's being overprotective toward you. If you discover you were correct in your evaluation, you're going to have to be understanding and forgiving toward him. I don't know what else to do. Being overprotective is not the worst flaw a father can have—it beats rejection any day. Still, it's bothersome. So talk with him about it.

Something else that bothers teens? If I could give one bit of practical advice to fathers, I would say, "Talk quieter." Here are four of my many "yeller" notes. I could have printed 400.

From Chicago: *"Heaven forbid if I tell my father that he's wrong, for his shouting isn't at all pleasant. It's one that could make the coolest person get goose bumps and a lump in their throat. He can make me cry by yelling no matter what the fight (normally one-sided) is about, big or little. Even many operations and a heart attack or dia-*

betes or the threat of high blood pressure will not keep him from yelling. I can't stop him."

From Seattle: "*My father started yelling at me for something insane (I moved his shoes!). This youth gathering is a place to get away from home. I haven't had a peaceful meal for nearly two weeks. This is heaven. Dad always yells at me. Why is he constantly yelling at me?*"

From Minneapolis: "*My father has a little trouble with his hearing and he always makes things out of what I say. He sort of fills in the words he didn't hear with his own and always does this for the worse. Then he yells and screams at me.*"

From Miami: "*My dad comes home in a bad mood and gets everyone else in a terrible mood and all we do is yell at each other.*"

Regardless of the reason, it's very difficult to discuss any issue when the participants, one or all, are yelling. Practical solution? Take all the "yelling subjects" to the smallest room in your house—the bathroom maybe. It's very hard to yell at people in a little room. Talk about going to a smaller room. Above all, don't introduce a "yelling subject" outside or in a large family room! Help your dad break that habit, and make sure you aren't just as guilty.

Pay attention to something else that surfaced in one of those notes: hearing. In our society many people work surrounded by excessive noise. Their hearing is damaged —they can't hear well. They get accustomed to shouting and do it automatically. Before you get too upset, figure out whether the real problem in your communication may be that dad needs a hearing aid.

Above all, don't yell back. Try this creative approach from a 15-year-old girl: "*My dad, when he comes home from work, he's usually tired and gripy. He works with a guy that complains and is always griping. When my mom and I ask him to do something, he starts yelling with a loud voice and starts getting mad at us. I sit there and call him "Fast Fuse" until I start making him laugh! DADS!!!*" Not everyone can pull that off, but if you can it's a very creative way to calm things down. Blessed is the yelling dad who has a sharp daughter like that.

Here's another problem: "*My dad travels the whole state so he isn't home much. I can't feel much affection for him.*" Young people are very conscious about fathers being gone a lot. A girl from Charlotte wrote: *"My dad's out of town too much with his job."* In these times, many fathers travel a lot. But have you ever wondered how often a father was gone from home 200 years ago? How long did it take to get to town or hunt for food or carry the crop to market? Many days. The absent father isn't something new. I know that won't make your situation any less painful, but it might help your perspective. Tell your dad how you feel. Maybe he'll take you with him sometime. Maybe he can shorten the amount of traveling he has to do. At least it will let him know that you care. You won't get him mad saying, "I sure miss you and wish you didn't have to be away so much." That kind of comment might help him make a decision he's been thinking about for a long time! However, don't forget that maybe the reason he's on the road so much is that you keep expressing needs which can't be satisfied any other way. He has to travel—for you! Most dads miss their children every bit as much as the children miss them. They just don't say it as often as they ought to. If you talk about it, everyone will be helped.

Are fathers consistent? Not at all. A 14-year-old boy wrote: *"I have had conflict with my father and he does things he tells us not to do. And I get mad because he gets mad at me."* Or how about this from a 17-year-old: *"My father is my employer and father. At work he treats me like an adult and at home treats me like a little kid and he can't tell the difference. What should I do?"*

Nobody tries to be inconsistent—it just develops naturally. Gently point out the contradictions in your father's behavior. Humor helps. A hug improves the situation as well. Be as kind in the correction of your father as you wish he would be with you. Use that standard as your guide. Sound familiar? Check out Matt. 7:12.

Here are more things that bother young people about their fathers: *"My dad always has to add his opinion to any and every subject, even if he doesn't have the slightest idea about what is going on."* *"Not being able to have a discussion with my father without having everything I say thrown back in my face. Example: 'That's a dumb idea.' How do you deal with that?!"* *"I have trouble talking with my father. He is fairly well known and highly educated and I feel the things that happen to me are so minor to him. I feel like a simpleton to him." "He talks too much and tells everyone how to do jobs (even when they know much more about the subject than he does). I hate to claim him when he says dumb things and wish I could disappear from sight then." "My dad is the world's best fault-finder I know—a few weeks ago he grounded me for two weeks because I would not button the second button of my shirt."*

Those are all important and painful teenage problems, especially when you love your father and want to honor him but don't know how (or why) to do it. Let me emphasize again the need to talk with him about your concern. Before you talk, try to figure out why he acts the way he does. Are you making something out of nothing? Sometimes people act toward others at home like they, in turn, are treated by others at their work. Is that possible with your dad? Sometimes overbearing people (dads included) are very insecure—yet all of us respond well to encouragement and affirming. Try it. A lot of dads are overwhelmed by the education of their sons and daughters and feel that *they* are inferior to their children. Some dads think they need to have *all* the answers. Talk to your father—or maybe talk about the problem with your mom. Get outside help for all of you where you can.

The tenderest area of relationship between a father and his children has to do with love. Here are some examples: *"It bothers me when my dad doesn't care enough about me to even know when I break my finger playing basketball, or when he finds out, he doesn't even show any sympathy." "My problem is my father. No matter how hard I try to make him proud of me, or have him show he cares for me at all, I get a negative reaction. I need help! The hurt that comes to me when I think of how much I love him and how little he seems to care is unbearable. He doesn't even seem to be aware of my presence. I'm going away to college soon and I need to know that I'm wanted somewhere." "I would love to get close to my father, but he comes from a home where no affection is shown. How can I get close to him?" "I get into quarrels with everybody, but after a while everything cools off. My father and I get along pretty well. Although we don't agree on everything, we normally reason things out." "How can I get a relationship with my dad? We've never been able*

to talk. I look at my friends and their fathers and how they talk and I want to do the same."

Did you recognize all the subtle differences in those messages? The problems are not exactly the same. Some hurts haven't been treated at all, others are pretty well worked out. But there is a common question. That question is, "What do you do when you love and don't feel good about the response you're getting?"

I'd suggest this—talk to your dad. If you can't talk to him, write him a note. Nothing beats person-to-person contact. Look for the best moment and place and mood to share. Try this approach: "Dad, I love you very much and I need to talk with you about something." Then talk. It may be that you've overreacted to his responses or misunderstood what he was trying to do. It's important to know that. In any event, you owe it to yourself and your father to try. Be loving, honest, and sensitive toward him. Don't attack him. Don't try to shame him. That won't work—it just gets people angry. Speak slowly and clearly. Listen carefully.

And if it doesn't work? You still have reaped a great benefit—you tried. You know you did. He knows you did. Maybe the stage is set for another day when your highest goal can be reached.

Mothers—God bless them too

What about mothers? For one thing, the concerns kids have about their mothers are not nearly as organizable as their feelings about their fathers. Feelings toward mothers flood out all over the emotional spectrum. Mother-feelings expressed by teenagers far outnumber the father-feelings expressed. That makes sense when you think about it. Most young people have more contact with their mothers than their fathers. So far, in our society, mothers do much more of the day-to-day listening, correcting, and instructing of children than fathers. This results in a different kind of reaction from the children.

Let's start with this problem. *"When I ask my mother if I can go someplace she says no and then my brother asks if he can go someplace and she says yes."*

Moms aren't consistent. It's even possible they have their favorites. But it's also possible that your mother gives special things to your brothers and sisters because those brothers and sisters, in that moment, need something special. Make sense?

A boy, 17, and a girl, 15, brought up that love problem again—it seems to affect relationships with mothers as well as fathers: *"My family has always been very cold. I'd like to express my feelings of love to my mother, but don't know how. I wish I knew how to reach her!"* and *"I want to show my mom my affection but she would think I was crazy."* If you want to show your mom you love her, go ahead and show her. If you want to say you love her, say it. How she reacts to your feelings is her problem. Expressing your feelings is yours. Follow your heart. It's not a promised easy road, but it certainly is the best road available to the caring person.

Among the most common concerns are these: *"What do you do about mothers who never listen to any of your questions?"* *"How can you get over the fear of talking over personal problems with ma?"* *"I don't seem to do anything right to please my mother. She doesn't realize how much I try to please her."* *"My mother is very edgy. She can become consumed with anger at the slightest provocation. She cannot relax. She wants to know where I've been every minute I'm out, and is always very suspicious."*

Those are all very heavy concerns. They express a lot of pain, yet they are healthy. Being able to analyze the problem is the first step toward a solution—even if the healing process hurts. The mother who was edgy and capable of sudden reaction was probably not feeling well physically. She may need medical attention. Teenagers can help parents by recognizing such signs. The 13-year-old who couldn't do anything to please her mother—or thought so—will have to say that to her mother sometime. It's a communication problem—the other two problems are of the same kind. If you're upset about something, you ought to say it, and hope mothers will listen.

You need to know that not every story has a happy ending, friends. Just like some parents have extremely difficult children, some children have extremely difficult parents. That's the way it works. If a difficult parent is the burden you must bear in life, then you ought to recognize it and handle it as best you can. Think of them

47

the same way you would if your parents were physically handicapped or the victims of some kind of accident. Make some allowances for them. Insert some adjustments in your life. When you need love and caring and encouragement, look around for other *good* places where you can find them. There are a lot of them. Not every great young person has great parents. It just doesn't work that way.

This next note contains an important message: Mothers, don't lie to your children or force your will on them—it builds distrust. A boy wrote: *"My mother is scissors crazy and she loves to cut my hair, and wants it her way, no compromise to it. I had long hair, very long hair, and she said, 'I'll only trim it one inch,' and she cut it to my ears. I just don't trust her anymore."* Short hair isn't a high enough price to get in return for a teenager's trust. That was a dumb mom.

Teenagers are softies. They care. They see things. They want to help. They appreciate being helped. Listen to these four notes:

"I was wondering why my mom forgave me so easily for something I think is very serious."

Moms forgive. They forgive because that's what we need, even when we don't deserve it.

"My mom always seems to get stuck in the middle of our problems by trying to help, and then gets blamed. I realize this but my older brother (19) doesn't and makes this worse by being insensitive to her."

Thank God she's trying. Thank God she's willing to get in the middle and get banged up. Now you have to watch out for her. Speak up on her behalf. Protect her in any way you can.

"Of all people, I tend to really pick on and verbally hurt my mother whenever I'm irritated. Sometimes I stop doing this because I know it sometimes really hurts. At most times we get along fine and are really close, but on occasion I have let her know that I enjoy the company of my father better which isn't true. So what can I do to stop saying things like this? I know it really hurts and I keep on doing it. So what can I do to have me stop?"

That writer has already taken the first step by analyzing the situation and admitting wrong. The next step is simpler yet. Stop hurting your mom. It's not a matter of will-power, it's a matter of *won't*power. There's no point in playing "poor me" when you're the one that made yourself poor. Cut it out. There's no reason you can't.

"Mostly it's my mom. My dad got laid up on the job and the reaction of the accident caused him to have diabetes. Now we have just mom working because my dad is 100% disabled, and my mom working full time for six children. The work is getting to her and besides special food for my dad. What can we do to keep mom from working so hard?"

That's a caring observation in a note from a girl, 14 years old. Sounds to me like the best thing to do is make sure no additional burdens fall on a hard-working mother. Take care of the cooking and cleaning and a lot of the family hassle, and do it as soon as possible. Kids can also find jobs to bring money home. That's no big deal. Lots of young people have financially helped their mothers and dads—and ought to continue doing so. Why should all the serving and the helping flow in one direction? Go get a job and bring in some cash. It won't kill you! There are plenty of homes that could not manage without the added income of some fine sons and daughters.

Parent problems need understanding

Top among solutions to parent problems is a key word: *understanding.* When a teenager of 13 wrote, *"My parents and I don't understand each other,"* she hit the nail right on the head. In almost every instance, both teenagers and parents—not just one or the other—carry the responsibility for inadequate understanding. Maybe as a teenager you can't handle your parent's problems, but you sure can work on your understanding of their problems. There are a lot of parent problems that need your understanding and aid.

Here's just such a problem expressed by a Baltimore girl: *"I would love for my parents not to fight."* Notes on that particular problem come in by the hundreds. What do teenagers need to understand where fighting between mom and dad are concerned? How about this: Parents have to work at their relationship with each other and some aren't very good at it! That's why the divorce rates are skyrocketing and family unrest seems to be at an all-time high. Sons and daughters need to understand that being married isn't easy. It's a hard job only made easier when husband and wife recognize the problem and really work together. Your parents have their hands full enough just being married—without adding the concerns that children bring! That's not an excuse for their fighting. It's an explanation. You need to understand that.

And here's something else both parents and teenagers need to understand. Teenagers are different from parents, and today's teenagers are different from yesterday's. One young man from Kansas City captured that thought in a sentence more profound than many of us realize: *There is a generation gap between me and my father—he doesn't understand me.* Whether your father and mother understand you or not, one thing is sure: There is a one-generation gap between you and your parents. A girl, 15, and a boy, 17, underline that thought: *"My parents always say 'When I was your age.' They were my age 30 years ago and I'm different from them." "My dad doesn't think like I do, and he thinks I don't deserve any more than he had when he was a kid."* See how it works? It's the generation gap that encouraged a wise young lady, 17, to say, *"My parents don't understand that I am my own person. They have to let me be the person I was meant to be and not the daughter they planned for me to be."* Read that last sentence again. I have never heard it put more beautifully. If it expresses your feelings, use it—adopt it as your own and let it help you in your "getting along."

How about this note? *"My mom doesn't believe anything I say. She has old-fashioned ideas, believing that high school is the same now as it was in 1955. What can I do to make her come into the present?"* Is anything older than you are "old-fashioned"? A 16-year-old thinks so: *"If I don't agree with my parents in a decision they think I'm wrong and tell me I'm very selfish and self-centered just because my opinions don't match theirs. They don't seem to realize that I don't want to think and act as old-fashioned as they do."*

One part of the solution to this problem is for everyone to realize that the world is different for each generation and must be seen as such. There isn't much point in discussing which era is better. It's enough to realize they are different, and then work it out from there. We must also realize that everyone—not just parents and not just teenagers, but everyone—will have to change in some way.

Change is possible and all right. Listen to this 16-year-old: *"It used to be my mom and dad wouldn't trust me. They still don't too much but it's getting better. Lately we've been talking. I really feel lucky to have parents that care!"* That's change. Change isn't fast, it's never total, it's seldom immediate. It takes time—just like growing up takes time for teenagers, growing up for parents takes time too. As a teenager, you didn't know everything that you know now from the day you were 13 on. You learned —a little at a time. Well, mothers and dads learn how to be parents of teenagers a little at a time as well.

How about realizing parents are getting older too? That means there are physical changes taking place in their bodies just like there are physical changes happening to you. You don't grow until you are 21 and then stay that way until you're 90. Every year in life brings physical, emotional, and mental changes and, as God wills, spiritual changes as well. Accept and rejoice in the possibility of change and help it happen for your parents. Recognize the possibility of change in yourself, and help it happen there as well.

There are many other problems with parents. A 19-year-old wrote, *"First there was a divorce of my parents. Second a real struggle with drug addiction and about what is sinful in a sexual relationship. In my family we talked a lot about my problems, but most of these fights turned into screaming matches, so I moved out to my own place."* Other teenagers wrote: *"I try to talk to my parents but they are never home."* Or, *"How can you get your parents to listen to your problems? I haven't lived up to their expectations in school."* Or, *"I can't talk to my parents—I don't think they trust me! ! I never see my dad because of school or work, and every time I try to talk to my mom she yells at me."* Or, *"My parents and I have a terrible relationship. I never see my dad because of school and work conflicting. Whenever I talk to my mom we argue sooner or later. The problem is I don't know if I want to bother to try and change the relationship between my parents and I."* Is a concern of yours on that list? The list could be so much longer, and it could include comments about many additional problems. But what about solutions? Aren't there any more solutions? Aren't there more ways to help teenagers get along with parents?

The answer is a giant-sized *YES!* Just listen to this. A 17-year-old boy from Seattle wrote, *"My parents took me out after church one Sunday to talk over a cup of cocoa. The conversation went precisely as I knew it would, rehashing the same problems and nothing was really settled. The only neat thing which came out during the conversation was when my dad compared talking to parents with praying. He said that a good Christian prays constantly not putting God in a closet for hard times, and that we should make an effort to talk about everyday things, not just hard problems."* See how it happened? All at once, a bit of solution surfaced. But how can you make it happen for you?

The first step toward making solutions happen is realizing how important it is to say and hear things like, "I love you," or "I forgive you." Those are crucial phrases in a Christian relationship. They get things going! And they are even more important in a non-Christian relationship where the love of Christ and his daily assurance of forgiveness is not clearly heard or hasn't been accepted. When that's the case, the love and forgiveness must be "lived out" by the Christian involved. These Christian young people make that point:

"Dad and I never had any father-son talks. I wish we would have. At 20 years old, I feel like I have lost out. I wish I could go back a few years and do a few things over." That's some statement! How about this? *"I love my family very much! I have only one problem. We get along very well! My dad lived in a very large family without a mom. Saying 'I love you' was hard for him and still is. It makes it hard for the whole family."* Or maybe this 15-year-old girl can help you see how important expressed love is with her comment: *"How does a person break the barrier of telling your family that you love them? Those words only pass between my parents."* Then there's this: *"I can communicate but not about love. I love my parents, but just can't tell them. I really need to."*

How do you get the love-talk going? It seems to me that you finally just have to start. Say to your mother and father that you want them to hear some words from you to them. That's not abnormal. Jesus called us to a life and a witness of the love and forgiveness we get from him. Those loving blessings come to us daily, at the point of our need and beyond! That's the first step—recognizing the need to say those words and wanting to say them.

Step two? After you realize the importance of expressing love, do it! Say those words out loud. But that, in turn, makes for all kinds of problems for some people. Which of the following circumstances fits your own personal love-communication problem? A Kansas City young man of 17 said, *"I can't discuss important matters with my folks because I get so upset I cry. Once we get talking, though, we're OK. How can we get started?"* Another asked this impossible but telling question, *"What can you do to improve communication, especially when someone's crabby?"*

Listen to this great question and think about it: *"As a parent, when you're talking to your daughters and they've done something to disappoint you and you ask your daughter where have we gone wrong in bringing them up, what do you expect to hear? All my friends' parents say that—and what are we supposed to say?"* One thing you can say to your mother or father is something loving like they haven't done anything wrong in rearing you. You might even say you think they've done a pretty good job. After that, talk about love—your love for them.

From Minneapolis the question, *"How can you make it easier to talk to your folks?"* And this one from a young man, *"My parents and I argue a lot, sometimes over nothing. I usually argue back, but a friend suggested just listening and not saying anything back. My father gets furious when I do that so I don't know what to do."* In that instance, I'm not sure what to do either, but I do know that a very bright 16-year-old has learned an awful lot to be able to write a sentence like that. Sometimes things don't work out immediately. Keep trying!

A girl wrote, *"How do you keep communication lines open in your family? What happens if there is talking, but members of the family make assumptions on what was actually said that shouldn't have been made? My father's definition of waiting is different than mine!"* Or from Minneapolis, a 17-year-old wrote, *"When I try to explain my actions to a problem to my mother she won't listen. She says she doesn't want to hear any more."* Here are two quick notes: *"I'm a 14-year-old and I had a small argument with my mother at a store when she laughed at a robe I tried on. I told her it bothered me and asked her to stop. She got mad and walked out. It wasn't anything terrible."* The terrible thing is that a mother misunderstood. *"How come most parents always think they're right and never give kids a chance to say how they feel about it?"*

All those notes are examples of communication problems. How many kinds of communication problems are there? Hundreds! But don't be overwhelmed by the number of them. Get your act together and learn how to work in that world of communications. Develop the skills. That brings us to step three.

Step one was to know the importance of saying I love you. Step two was to say it. Step three is to learn how to say it well.

You have to realize you can't communicate very effectively when you're crabby. Remember that note? And you have to understand that parents generally believe they are right. Realizing things like that is part of learning the skills of communication. We all must find ways to speak so that others can understand. When you are a teenager, some of the "others" are your parents!

Let's try a few real-life problems. See how well you do. See if you can't figure out a good answer, and then think about how you would say it—and say it *well*. Start with this one: *"Whenever my parents and I discuss something they say their piece and tell me that the subject is closed. They feel that I should have no say in anything we discuss. Is there any way I can change them or me so that things work out better?"*

That's a good question. Did you develop an answer? Here's mine: By the time you're 16, you should have the right to talk with your parents. But you also ought to be old enough to recognize that when things aren't working well in one way, you ought to try working things out another way. Find the best moment for sharing—the moment when things are most tranquil and most open to communication. Then speak up like the adult you are rapidly becoming. Don't whine. Don't shout. Don't plead.

Don't cry. Say something like this, "I'm really growing up quickly. Before long I'll be 17 and soon after that, 18, and very quickly, 21. I have all kinds of decisions to make and I need someone to discuss them with. I'd like to discuss them with you. But discussing them means that we both have to talk. Will you talk things over with me? I need that." Be very gentle when you say that, but say it.

Ready for another try? *"What do you do if your parents are wrong and you know you are right?"* What do you say? It depends on the seriousness of the subject—and the kind of relationship you have with your mom and dad. You should never belittle your parents or demean them. How about saying something like, "You probably didn't know this, because if you had I'm sure you would have said something different, but I found out the other day that . . . ." If it's just a matter of opinion, don't fuss much. There's no point arguing about opinions. The same applies if it's a matter of taste. But if it's a matter of facts, then speak right up. However, do so as gently as you can.

What about this? *"It always seems that I end up in an argument with my parents. It seems that they say that I have to change my ways. I tried to talk to them about it, but it doesn't seem to work. What should I do?"* Won't it depend on the matter being discussed? Maybe you *will* have to change. Parents aren't always right, but they aren't always wrong either. I suspect that parents are more often right than wrong. Yet you still ought to have the right to talk about it. Ask for that right.

Here are two stimulators for developing your communication skills. *"How can you talk to your father and mother if you know already they're gonna object to what you're gonna say?"* And, *"I sometimes never get a chance to explain myself."*

In the second example, a skill in explaining is required. I believe in the phrase, "Writing maketh an exact man." That means when you write things down, you usually express yourself more clearly than when you just start talking. More than that, a written message gives the person you're communicating with a chance to think before reacting. So what about writing a note? Or how about asking for two uninterrupted minutes to make your case?

The first note sounds like there is some kind of basic conflict, either between the parents and the teenager, or maybe just conflict between generations. If you know that someone is going to object immediately, then your problem is learning to converse when you are beginning with a basic disagreement. That's very hard to do—but it's not impossible. When there is fundamental disagreement, start with prayer. Ask God to give winsome words and clear speech and ask for the same gifts for the other person as well! Then ask that God give everyone open minds and ears eager to hear. Finally, ask for the capacity to say things with such kindness and caring that the communication process is lubricated.

We know, as Christians, that no one is perfect. Not teenagers, not parents. We have no right to expect others to be perfect, and we have no right to let others expect us to fulfill that impossible expectation. Forgive yourself for your failures in communication as you do for anything else. Christ teaches us that! Then forgive your parents for the same failures.

My final word of encouragement: Work at improving the situation you find yourself in. Develop the skills for getting along with others and speaking so that others can hear. Those are the same skills you will need as an employee or as a partner in marriage. Start developing those abilities while you are a teenager!

Meanwhile you're going to change, and change a lot, during the passing of years. Don't automatically resist change. Some change is important for growing up. But you also want the presence of the Lord in your life so you can weigh the potential change against his Word, and against his will for you. If it fits comfortably, make the shift. If it doesn't, say no.

Most young people eventually grow up and leave home. How well they do living away from home is largely determined by how well they lived with their parents during their developing years, at least at first. While you still have those years, build the kind of memories that only get better with the passing of time. The teenage years are great years for getting along—with your parents.

FOUR

Getting Along
with Brothers and Sisters
and Some Other
Close Relatives

When brothers and sisters, in any number and in any combination, live out their lives together under one roof, at least a *little* conflict can be expected. This conflict can be funny to read about: *"I have a problem with my sister. She is a clean freak! She's always taking my things and putting them away. And often after that I can never find it. And when I ask her where it is she goes crazy. What should I do?" "I had a conflict with my sister because we sing together and my voice hasn't matured yet and she gets mad because I can't sing high."*

Some teenagers are wisely analytical about conflict with brothers or sisters. *"My brother and sister were arguing when they were tired. Their argument was stupid. They would never act that way outside the family, but only within the family." "How do you get along with a sister very similar to yourself—stubborn?"*

A number of reports about family conflict are very troubled, like this comment from a Kansas teenager: *"We fail to build each other up; instead we constantly put each other down. Somebody is always criticizing or complaining—even after church on Sunday, just as if nobody caught the message in pastor's sermon, or even felt the love of God. This is destroying any love and happiness present in our family."*

And then there are observations about conflict that suggest a history of hassle but also still communicate a desire to continue helping: *"How do you be stern and yet not a pushover with a little brother or sister?"*

Reading through my pile of notes and letters convinces me that there are a lot of homes where resolving difficult relationships between brothers and sisters is the number one need. The desire to resolve that tension is good. Left unattended, struggles between brothers and sisters can turn into 20th century Cain and Abel situations (Genesis 4)—it can get *that* bad. More likely, though, antagonism will stop far short of murder and rather settle down to an annoying and persistent level of bickering, sniping, fussing, arguing, nagging, irritating, and other less dramatic family reactions. But they aren't really less serious! Those troublesome snipings peck away at unity, at fun, at loving, and at caring. They erode the very meaning of the word *family*. They attack Christ's intent that each of us have an abundant life (John 10:10). Family conflict is a serious matter!

Am I exaggerating? Am I distorting reality? Listen to four teenagers, ages 14, 15, 16, and 17, who don't think so.

One: *"Since my mother has been going to school and working regular hours, I am left to make dinner and care for my brothers and sisters. Whenever I tell my brothers or sisters not to do something or to do something they run and call dad saying I am hurting and literally beating them when I haven't even touched them. My dad doesn't listen to my story and tells me to leave them alone. My mom will finish school this year so it should be better."*

Two: *"My mom and my brother don't get along very well. He's away at college but when he comes home they still fight. Constantly. I'm the youngest and everything they yell about reflects on me and I want my mom and brother to get along but what can I do? Should we go to a family counselor?"*

Three: *"I'm the oldest of out of five kids in my family. I don't really know my family and they don't really know me. We fight, get jealous of each other, and worst of all don't show we love each other. This makes me sick. I don't know what a real family is. How can we become one? I am a 16-year-old girl."*

Four: *"I can't argue sensibly without having a fight with family members. Everyone does it—all of us."*

This kind of serious conflict involving brothers and sisters is the subject of most of this chapter. First we're going to focus on brothers, then we're going to spotlight sisters. I will also include a few paragraphs about another part of many families: grandparents.

Brothers

Let's begin with two notes about brothers, one from a boy and the other from a girl: *"My brother and I just don't get along. He has a terrible temper and we argue if we just look at one another. We really don't have any good reason to argue—so why do we?"* *"My brother is very involved in his own affairs and he doesn't care about our family, but we care about him, but it doesn't get through."*

How would you respond to those notes? The first note makes me wonder whether *both* boys don't have a terrible temper. It's hard to argue with yourself. Both must be at least a little involved. While I don't know what these two argue about, I do know the first step toward final resolution of a problem is recognizing shared responsibility for that problem.

The other note reminds me to repeat this fact: Most problems don't get settled very quickly. It takes a long time for a family problem to develop; it takes a long time for people to recognize and define that problem; finally, it takes a long time to work out a suitable solution and then implement it. Family living requires longtime commitments! There are few quick, easy answers, but there *are* answers. Those who seek will find the solid answers their situation requires. In the process of resolution, they may also find happiness, joy, and a lifetime of pleasure. The resolution of conflict is really worth the effort.

Let's get back to brothers. Brothers come in two varieties—older and younger. Each variety has its own set of tensions and each creates its own kinds of concerns. Here are four letters that have to do with Type A—*younger* brothers.

"My little brother is a loner. He is always feeling sorry for himself and he's always trying me (I have a temper

59

too). When I lose my temper you'd better watch out. So I always get blamed for what he does. What should I do?"

All brothers have ways of testing, trying, and teasing one another. It's normal. Little brothers seem to do more and be better at it than older ones. Part of the reason for that is little brothers want to do and be what older brothers and sisters have already done and now are—only quicker! They want the older brother's rights and experiences much sooner than their "seniors" had them. The family task is to keep those normal urgings to grow up within creative channels and controlled in an orderly process of development.

It's easiest to fight or argue or try settling disagreements by force. But these approaches don't settle things for very long. A higher goal is to figure out ways of helping that don't just make more waves! Learning how to do this—to deal with the younger brother or sister in a positive way—is a continuing process. In the process you develop skills and abilities that will serve you well all life long. Think about it that way. Then keep on trying to find ways to help your brother or sister grow up—if possible—better and easier than you did!

"I have a problem with my little brother. He's very stuck on himself. He won't listen to me even though I'm older than he is. He thinks he can do everything in the world. Just a pain in the butt."

I wonder if his little brother feels the same way about him? Wouldn't you guess that the little brother is not as interested in doing "everything in the world" as he is in doing everything his older brother does? If you have a problem like this one, a good way to handle it is to talk to your folks about developing a few boundaries around your "older" life so that you can have some privacy. It's OK to do that. But you must also remember that your younger brother needs good experiences with people your age. He needs to tag along sometimes. You can really help if you let him. With your aid, that younger brother can become something better than he ever would be if left to himself. If the older brother in our example would help his little brother, it just might be that the focal point of his feelings toward his little brother might shift up his own anatomy to his heart and, in the process, change from pain to love.

60

"I'm much bigger than my younger brother, but he is always calling me names and putting me down. It's hard to fight off the urge to hit him."

Fight it off anyway. Force only triggers more force. Those who hit get hit. But more important—force doesn't work. Try the Jesus method. He said, "Love your enemies and pray for those who persecute you" (Matt. 5:44). He was also talking about people who irritate you. The Jesus approach helps the other guy change. When people change, they don't act in the old ways anymore. Don't hit! Help!

"My younger brother (age 12) and I despise the mere sight of each other. Why? Because for so many years I was 'mother' to my brother while mom worked, and it's hard for me to drop that attitude and he resents my mothering."

The young lady who wrote that note is a sharp cookie. She has the matter perfectly analyzed. Now all she has to do is implement a proper solution. As a first step, she must stop mothering. One mother at a time is enough. What her younger brother needs is not another mother, but a sister. She must be that sister and give him room to grow.

Similarly troublesome situations come with older brothers. The first common older brother problem isn't really a problem of the older brother. Read it and see if you agree. *"My brother is in college and he gets most of the attention."*

I wonder if the writer of that sentence isn't the one who has the problem? Maybe the older brother actually does get most of the attention, but the more serious problem (at least for the writer) is what the younger brother will do about it. When someone else's action, intentional or unintentional, can make you feel bad—look out! Satan uses that as a way to make your heart his home. Real bitterness between brothers and sisters quickly develops over a statement like, "Mother always liked you best." Maybe she did, maybe she didn't—that's not the point. The point is how you deal with that real (or imagined) concern.

Here are two similar older-brother problems. *"My brother because he is older than me thinks he can boss me around all the time." "My brother who is older than* me always pushes me around. He told his friend that he hates me, and I eventually found out."

Whether that undesirable quality is called "bossing" or "pushing," it still isn't a very nice thing to have happen to you. The best thing to do is to look your older brother in the eye and say, "When you push me around it's very difficult for me to like you. It makes me wonder whether you like yourself." That could make your older brother think—and maybe change. I'd use the same approach with anyone who said they hated me. Of course, find out first if your actions might have stimulated that response in him. *Then* talk about the action and the reaction. Change yourself if that is needed. Ask your brother to change as well. Go to someone else—a teacher, your dad, a cousin, a friend—for help in making a brother change. It's a great way to help changes happen and can end up as a mighty blessing for both.

A young man from Kansas City had this problem: "*My problem is my oldest brother. He no longer lives at home, but when he did, we only fought. Usually about the way he treated my parents. He lives far away and now I have told him I love him, but he doesn't really respond. What can I do?*" Go back to the point I made earlier: Some things need time for change. Some people change or respond quickly, others very slowly. We must be ready to reach out again and again in love toward a person, but there are no guarantees that the other person (it doesn't have to be a brother) will respond to your loving action either in the way or as quickly as you want. No guarantees at all. That doesn't relieve you of the responsibility for exerting the loving action.

What do you do if you don't get the response you expect? Keep at it. Love some more, and then some more. Reflect the patient persistent love of Christ. Don't give up. Try and try and try again. Then try once more. That's what Christ did and still does for us.

I don't know whether the following notes reflect older brother or younger brother problems, but check them over and see if they might be familiar and whether you have any answers. "*My brother always picks constantly about my height, then he gets everyone else picking on me. I don't mind being picked on, but after awhile it turns into a fight.*" "*My brother makes a fool of himself which in* turn offends me. He has some strange habits which turn other people off toward me. I like him but he sometimes offends my friends in front of me." "My brother and I don't get along because he doesn't think I'm good enough for him." "My brother gives me an inferiority complex. He's always calling me stupid, totally unprovoked."

As a thought-starter for approaching these concerns, remember the old saying: "You can pick your friends, but you can't pick your relatives."

The best approach to brother and sister tensions is a one-to-one talk. Don't begin by telling your opposite what won't work or what isn't right or what you demand or what you won't stand for. Don't shout. Don't slam things. Don't cry. Don't threaten. Don't insult. Talk calmly. Keep a low voice. Look at the other person eye-to-eye. The sooner you do it, the better. More than that, the sooner you do it, the quicker all those wonderful "together days" from which family memories are woven can be claimed. Nothing beats loving conversation for clearing the air and healing all wounds! Get going at it—now!

Sisters

Conflict between or with sisters is different from conflict with brothers. Brothers hit and push and shove—they are much more physically aggressive. At least that's what I read in the letters I received. Sisters hurt others in a more subtle fashion—they conduct a war of nerves. It's not a physical battle. They wear away on others. Many family members accused sisters of "bugging." Isn't that a fascinating word? A 14-year-old simply reported, *"My sister bugs me."* A 16-year-old put it this way, *"My sister bugs me to no end. She finds something wrong with everything I do. She is good to my mom but behind her back she is a real bugger. She's 14."*

Sisters seem to have a variety of bugging methods. Any effective means of irritating another apparently qualifies for that descriptive tag. It can be as basic as, *"My 10-year-old sister is so lazy she refuses to work,"* or as all-inclusive as, *"My sister and I fight about anything but everything."* It can even be as emotionally painful as, *"Fighting with my sister really isn't fighting. It's more like black-*

mail. I'm very loyal to her but she uses me. I try to give her unconditional love but she throws it back in my face. It hurts me. My solution is either leave or give up completely." Those three notes signify significant tension in varying degrees of intensity and in an interesting variety. All are hard to live with and must be faced.

While specific problems vary between brother-conflict and sister-conflict, the solutions always flow from the same beginning steps. The first step is a willingness to determine, to the satisfaction of all concerned, what the actual problem is. Second, there must be a commitment to talk with each other. Only then is help possible.

Sisters, like brothers, come in two varieties: older and younger. Here are some "younger sister" notes and comments.

A 16-year-old girl wrote, *"My little sister is constantly getting into trouble, but she pulls me into it. She says that it's my fault. I get blamed. Mom says I should set a good example, only I didn't have anything to do with it. What should I do?"*

Have you ever noticed that little sisters and parents seem to be natural allies—and older sisters the enemy? I really think parents agree with little sisters more than they do with their older sons and daughters. The older ones are expected to be good examples and active guardians. To a degree that is a real necessity and should be expected—but not always. Little sisters need to grow up too. They need a chance to make mistakes; they need to be given responsibility and then be held accountable for what they do. They need some correction. You older sisters and brothers gently share that with your folks— and with your little sisters. Talk about it with your folks, particularly if your little sister is constantly manipulating a situation to her own advantage. That kind of action is fairly common and bad news. Help her stop that pattern as early in life as possible. It will be a blessing! But, in doing so, make sure you aren't just trying to avoid responsibility yourself!

A 20-year-old tells this story: *"There's conflict between me and my sister, nine, about the lies and stories she tells."*

Does it sound dumb for a grown-up man to talk about a nine-year-old sister that way? Dumb or not, it's real, and it's quite a common matter. Tension between brothers and sisters is not limited to certain ages, especially when the tension is over one of the age "equalizers" like lying. A lie hurts a person of any age and can be spoken by a person of any age. Those early lying practices must be confronted and exposed. There'll be no peace in the family until they are faced firmly. To help the liar change, the treatment must be done in a way that teaches and "tames" through learning. During the process of confrontation, forgiveness must be freely and continually offered. Yet it can only be claimed when the liar genuinely confesses and asks for help. Be as loving and tender with "sinners" as was Christ, and just as patient with them. But be just as firm too!

A 15-year-old girl was upset because *"when my younger sister does something wrong it's my fault because my sister is supposed to have picked it up from me."*

That would upset me too. Yet we must remember that other people, little sisters included, *do* imitate. They watch and then mimic. Even if we don't try to teach younger ones wrong things, they still learn. If we are the "teacher," we are at least partly responsible for what the other person "learns." Be sensitive about your example! Make it a good one. People learn from our good examples just as easily as our bad. Let your good light shine before your little sister. That will help you both.

Two girls, one 17 and one 16, unrelated and separated by a continent, make these interestingly similar comments: *"My younger sister wants to do more than I can. She is 15. What shall I do?"* *"My younger sister is 13 and she honestly (and not because I'm feeling sorry for myself) doesn't have to do any work around the house that I had to do when I was her age."*

I'm always intrigued how often older sisters or brothers think that all younger sisters and brothers are spoiled and should not receive any more than they got when they were their age. Is that true? One of the earliest discoveries of life is that fairness doesn't mean gifts or abilities must be equally distributed. It doesn't happen that way. Some people are smarter than others. Some are prettier. Some are stronger. Some are richer. Some are more personable. Life is often unequal, and so is living together in your house. People have different needs at different times.

Younger sisters won't be required to do all the things that older sisters did, and it's just as true that older sisters will not be doing all the things that younger sisters do. The circumstance of the family changes. Financial conditions vary from year to year. Parents have improved understandings of what is correct from time to time.

If you feel cheated about the way someone else is treated in your family, talk to your folks. Say something like this, "I don't like the way I feel, but I think if I could talk with you it would help. I always have the feeling that I'm not getting the same things that my brothers or sisters are getting. . . ." That's a good way to open a conversation about this problem. Be sure you're prepared for your parents' answers! Most parents are much fairer than their kids think. You may discover that you've overlooked a number of things or didn't realize some basic facts.

Now let's examine some of the things that bother people about older sisters. Three boys had these things to say about their older sisters: *"My sister is a senior and she tries to be my mother." "When my sister comes home mother turns me into a servant." "My older sister moves so slow in the morning that she always makes me late for school (I ride in her car with her)."*

The first two situations call for confrontation. Talk about the problem. The last statement sounds like part of the fun of life. You will discover that in areas where there are no scriptural rights or wrongs, you may often be linked with people with whom you disagree or who do things differently than you would like. They probably won't change, so why not relax. But determine that when you get older, you're not going to act that way. That would be quite a powerful learning for life!

A 14-year-old young lady wrote a long letter: *"It seems sometimes I can't get along with my sister. She always makes me out to be wrong all the time. I try to talk to her but she doesn't want to listen. I want to get along with her. I try. What should I do? I'm not always right, I do have faults, but I just can't win! I don't mean winning the argument, but just getting along with her is hard sometimes. She's older than I am, and it seems she just won't let me grow up in my own way! Sometimes when she finds something funny and I don't laugh she gets mad and says, 'What's wrong with you?' It's like I have to laugh. Maybe I found it funny, but didn't laugh. Maybe I didn't think it was funny! I try to tell her to run her own life and let me grow up, but she just shakes her head and laughs at me.*

If younger sisters have an inclination to manipulate others, older sisters have an inclination to dominate others. Neither is a very loving thing to do. Time could take care of the problem, but why wait? Talk about it now. Remember how to talk: calmly; low voice; no tears; factually; with love; toward a mutually acceptable solution.

This 15-year-old girl has a different problem. *"I can't handle my sister. She's 16 and I'm her slave. When she gets mad I get the flak and I hold back my temper. What should I do when I want to hit her back?"*

Don't. Jesus was right. Those who use force get force used on them (Matt. 26:52). That's just *one* good reason for not hitting. A better one is that love won't allow it. Be patient, tender, gentle, understanding. In other words, keep your cool. Take a walk when you're steaming! If you need to "get back at her," do it by the legitimate means of confrontation and direct discussion. That method might not change things immediately, but it will surely set the stage so that things can finally be changed.

Here are a series of additional sister situations.

1) *"My sister always yells at me whenever she brings home a friend and I spend more time with her friend than she does."*

I'd yell at you too. When your sisters or brothers bring home a special guest, the best thing you can do is make some polite conversation and then disappear, unless you are clearly invited to stay. The 14-year-old brother who wrote the note is butting in—no doubt about it.

2) *"I argue with my sister a lot. Sometimes we get into really bad fights. I wish we wouldn't fight, but it seems my sister makes me blow up and I get mad."*

I don't believe that. Other people don't get you mad. Other people do some things and then you get yourself mad. Don't do it. Control that over which you actually have control—yourself.

3) *"My sister said that I think I know everything."*

I wonder why she'd say that? Could it be this brother projects an all-knowing image? Much of the time there's at least a seed of truth in the criticisms people make about us. Better look in the mirror and find out if it's true. If it's not true, maybe you can say to your sister, "If I really knew everything, I would know why you're saying I know everything—and I don't." Then talk. If it is true, change.

4) *"The source of difficulty with my sister is her lying and stealing from other members of the family."*

That's very serious. Stealing from a family member is common, but still inexcusable. The same goes for lying. When things like that are happening, the family is in real trouble. Yet, before you make a charge against anyone, *be sure you have the facts.* Suspicion that someone is doing something is not the same thing as proof. When you have the full facts, confront the person privately. If that doesn't change matters over a period of time, then talk to your parents. Lying and stealing are serious matters that have to be dealt with.

5) *"My sister and I are about the same age and we can't get along at all. She's always been slow at learning so my mom really babies her. I get the blame for most everything because of this and sometimes I feel like just walking out. What can I do?"*

It sounds like while one sister gets babied, the other one is the baby. By the time you're 17, you ought to recognize a lot of the important things about life. One of them is that "exceptional" people need some kind of exceptional care. I'm wondering if the writer would be willing to trade places with her less-gifted sister. Don't ask for "equal treatment" (whatever that means) in what is obviously an *un*equal situation. Thank God for the special gifts you have, and see if you can't come to a better understanding about that special treatment someone else seems to be getting—and probably needs.

6) *"There is a conflict between me and my sister because we are so different and have completely different interests. We seem unable to accept each other's faults and are constantly getting on each other's nerves."*

That's a perceptive observation for a 15-year-old. She said, "We seem unable to accept each other's faults . . ."— that means she knows she has them. Hooray for her! Knowing that much means the day of resolution is not far away.

That's a good closing point to make: There is always a day of resolution. There always comes a time when those old hurts and feelings get confronted and, hopefully, resolved. Look around at your aunts and your uncles and other older folks. Do you realize they struggled with each other in the past just as intensely as you and your family members do now? Some of them never learned to stop. That's why there is tension at many family gatherings and why some close relatives avoid each other. Too bad! But that's not the way it works out with most people. Most people settle their differences sooner or later. Why wait for later? Why not settle them sooner, and begin the happy business of living the joyful life with each other right now?

You and your sisters *are* different. But different doesn't mean better, it just means different. Accept those differences which are proper, legitimate, and normal—and praise God for them. Then help each other correct those differences that are flaws and that tear down families. Help stop the lying, manipulating, dominating, stealing, and using. Begin with yourself. Then reach out to do what you can for your brothers or sisters. You'll like yourself more for trying. You'll like your brothers and sisters more as you succeed. Doesn't that make the effort worth exerting?

Grandparents

Grandparents are not parents. Grandparents are not sisters or brothers. Grandparents are grandparents. They're something special and often very close. They are part of many families. Sometimes they live in your home. Sometimes they live next door. Sometimes they live a long way off, but very often they have a direct influence on family living.

There are great advantages to having grandparents around. They bring an experience and a calmness that's very helpful and can do a lot to reinforce and give support to young people. But like with mothers, fathers, sisters, and brothers, there can be some problems with grandmothers and grandfathers as well. Many of these problems affect teenagers. Here are some notes that illustrate what I mean.

70

"*What do you do if your grandpa and your father are comparing you with your great-grandma who was a very devout Christian and you haven't committed your life to Christ?*" I'm not going to touch the last part because that would need some personal contact. But the first part of that note surfaces a common problem in life: comparing. It's very difficult for many people to resist comparing, especially as they get older. What's more difficult yet is comparing accurately. All of us have a tendency to make the past very perfect while dramatizing all the flaws of the present. You have to take many of the comments grandparents make about specific instances in the past with a grain of salt. They aren't lying—they just don't recall clearly. Don't let anyone force a standard or a comparison or an attitude of the past on you without a lot of factual support for it and, most important, without your permission. Stand your ground, even with grandparents. Tell them all that might have been very true, but it's not where you're at. That's the best and most honest way to deal with them.

"*My grandpa is 91 years old and lives with our family for six months out of every year. While he is there my mom is his daughter and waits on him. But she also has the pressure from my father, who feels neglected, and the rest of my grandpa's kids hardly ever come to see him. When they do, it's for an afternoon and really short. For the other six months he's at his other daughter's house. My mom is dead set against having him go to a nursing home and my dad can't understand this. I'm just stuck in the middle loving both parents and grandpa. What can I do to help relieve the pressure?*"

That story is one that is repeated over and over again. I believe the husband is correct in his attitude. There's only one lasting relationship in life: marriage. God spells it out and makes that primary relationship very clear (Gen. 2:24). If the husband and wife agree on how the wife will treat the grandfather, that's one thing. But if she forces her will and attitude about her father upon her husband, that's something else, and it's wrong. Sounds to me like the wife, in this instance, has forgotten she's married. Husbands can do the very same thing. Someone in the family needs to speak to the real issue, and that has to do with relationships. Rather than stand in the middle, see if you can't get everyone out of that muddle with some clear direction from Scripture. Talk about it!

"I love my grandma a lot, but she tries to run my father's life and the whole family's life. She is so thoughtless of others, she only thinks about herself." "The conflict is with my grandma, because she has lived with our family my whole life, and has been a second mother to me, and I resent her telling me what to do." "My biggest problem is my grandmother. She lives next door and spends all day at our house. My parents pay her for cooking our meals. I resent her for this because I make meals too and don't get paid (no allowance). All she does is yell at me and my brother from the minute we walk in the door until sleep. We are often very tired from school and then she yells at us to do something for her. If we tell her we are tired and can't we do it later, she tells us 'How can you get tired from school?' And all she does is sit on her rear all day and do nothing and then she tells us how much she does for us and how little we do and what lazy slobs we are."

All three of those look like problems with dominating grandmas. Or maybe parents have laid aside their responsibilities and passed the buck to grandma. Like every other problem in life, the solution flows from a Christian confrontation. I'd start by talking with grandma. If that doesn't work, talk to your parents. It's obvious that having one mother and one father at a time is enough for any youngster. No substitutions are really possible. The best grandma and best grandpa are those who are the grandma and grandpa.

"My widowed grandmother has problems facing my grandfather's death." Death is a very fundamental part of life. Facing the death of a loved one is an equally fundamental part of life. Helping someone face the death of a loved one is also very important. That's where you come in. Help by understanding that everyone works out their grief in a different fashion. Some cry a lot. Others are depressed. Some immerse themselves in work. Others do a lot of remembering. There are varieties of initial reactions. Help that grandmother or grandfather work through their grief toward positive Christian goals. Depending on the seriousness of the situation, you may want to suggest some sort of professional assistance. In any eventuality, lend your ear and give comfort with your presence. Listen and let them unload their feelings. You will discover helping them will help you face similar circumstances later in your life.

Conflicts that pop up between grandparents and others can have to do with very minor details or very serious concerns. Whatever the case, the conflicts need to be discussed and worked out openly. There is no other satisfactory way of resolving them. People over 70 can be just as reasonable—or just as unreasonable—as teenagers. Talk about it—OK?

Most of the illustrations here point toward grandmothers. Does that mean that grandfathers aren't problems? Not at all. What it means is that there are more grandmothers than grandfathers. Women outlive men, so in life's later years there are many more women than men. The majority of problems with grandparents will naturally focus on grandmothers—but only because of the law of averages.

Let me repeat this: Grandparents are really superspecial people. They give so much and take so little. If you would give more to them, you would get more from them. Regardless, share with them your understanding, your respect, your love, and your care. That's the way to honor your grandfather and grandmother and practice the positive respect God desires of you for them.

The amount of time in your life which you spend in your parents' home is really quite short compared with the total years you live. That period during which you have conscious relationships with sisters and brothers is shorter yet. But you will still have those sisters and brothers long after you have all left your parents' home. Treasure them as God's great gifts. They are a continuing lifelong source of help, advice, support, encouragement, love, and protection. Build good relationships with them now. All it takes is a modest amount of effort. You will bless the day you decide to treasure your brother or sister as highly as you do your friends. When you do, they end up being among those whom you call your *best* friends.

FIVE

Getting Along
with Your Friends—
Both Male and Female

Friends are important. But it's not easy to get friends—or keep them. A North Carolina 16-year-old put it this way: *"The thing that is bothering me most is making and improving friendships."* A Texas teenager pointed out some of the problems that surface while making friends when he asked, *"When you're trying to make new friends or start new relationships, what do you talk about? Yourself? What if you can't find anything to say about yourself? Then what? If you'd like to join in on a discussion and can't think of anything to say, what do you do?"*

Those two examples demonstrate that "friending" isn't easy! Getting and keeping friends is one of the greatest and most important challenges a teenager faces. This chapter will deal with getting and keeping friends—all kinds of friends.

Just friends

I'm a pastor. When I interview a couple prior to marriage, I generally ask them how many friends they have. Invariably they answer my question with another question: "What kind of friends do you mean? Do you mean good friends or real good friends or just friends?"

What a fascinating response! People seem to think that there are all kinds of friends. They don't discriminate between friends and acquaintances, but try to bunch everyone under the umbrella term *friends.* In the process they dilute the word's meaning. The reason I ask the young couples about friends is that I want to help them realize they don't really have many friends. No one does. It's not that they (or we) aren't popular. It's not that they aren't likable. The truth is that none of us has time to make and keep a whole lot of friends. Developing and maintaining friendships takes time. You and the other person or persons have to share experiences, need time for long talks together, must have opportunities to discover your commonalities and your likes and dislikes. All that takes time—hours, weeks, months, years. So my first-basic point is that *no one has a lot of friends*—there's not enough time! There's no need to be concerned if you feel close to only one or two people. Actually, three good friendships is about all one person can keep going at any one time.

The second basic point about friendships is that *any relationship which requires constant agreeing or giving in isn't worth having.* Relationships which are developed under those conditions aren't real. They appear for a while and are gone at the first little puff of conflict or chance for a more profitable relationship. Don't give up anything of value—moral or otherwise—as price for friendship. That price is too high. Let a friendship develop, but let it exist on the basis of an equal sharing and acceptance of one another.

The third basic point is that the best way to get a friend is by being one. Do friendly things! But in choosing which friendly things you want to do, resist heavy-handed peer pressure. Peer pressure is that force that you feel pushing at you from people around you (your classmates, those who live in your neighborhood) to do something you don't really want to do or wouldn't do voluntarily. Peer pressure doesn't always urge you to do something morally wrong. Maybe it only presses you to do something you think is dumb or inconsistent with your character. Resist that. Sometimes you simply can't go along with the others, including someone with whom you want to be close. Don't worry. Just about the time you feel you're left out, you'll discover that there are others—many others —who feel the same way as you do, but who are waiting for someone with the courage to state their feelings. Be yourself. Anything else is dishonest. Let other people be themselves as well.

Sometimes there is a pressure inside you to do weird things. Just listen to this Virginia Beach, Virginia, young lady: *"My biggest problem is that when I try to be nice to people, it always turns out wrong, and I end up being nasty toward them."* Or how about the message from this St. Louis young man, *"My mom says if I act the way I act at home to my friends, I won't have any."*

There are other times that *you* act all right, but your friends do strange things! A 17-year-old from Seattle wrote, *"Why do the things my friends do drive me up the wall?"* A 15-year-old from Atlanta is just as upset, *"What disturbs me is the way some people treat others—sometimes it's cruel."* Is it possible that you and your friends together are a real pain? One note read, *"My friends and I are cliquish."*

Friends don't always act with sensitivity. This note came to me at a youth gathering: *"We have a problem. Two of our friends are going together (a boy and a girl) and they are always together. Everyone is sick of it, including his parents and family. The girl and I used to be super friends but we never get a chance to talk anymore. She doesn't even know I got a ring from my boyfriend for Christmas, and they're here at this gathering with us."* That's sure some friends isn't it? And how about this, *"Why do all my friends ignore me or change the subject when I want to talk about my work with retarded children?"*

Friendships can put you in a bind of not knowing how you really feel. A college student wrote, *"How can I love the girl living across the hall in my dorm when everything she says and does irritates me? I know the problem is my attitude, but how can I change?"*

Then there are those disappointing moments when you don't know how to act responsibly to a friend. Two 16-year-olds wrote, *"The thing that bothers me most in my life right now is the jealousy I feel toward my best friend,"* and *"Why is it that I can never give people helping words when they are depressed and really need advice and are asking for it? I have prayed so much about it and it seems like I never think of anything reassuring to give. It's not* that I don't have enough faith in God and think that he wouldn't help me, because I do believe he will support me in anything like that, but I pray so hard he will make the right words come out so I can help this person, because I don't want to give the wrong advice or help. How come I can't find the right answers? It makes me so mad because many people have come to me for advice and feel confident in me and trust me, but I get so depressed and mad when I can't find the right words. I want to help."

All these examples demonstrate it isn't easy to have or be a friend. Knowing that, I still say: Go ahead and make the effort! That's my fourth basic point about friendship. *Realize that friendships require effort on the part of all concerned.*

When the object of the friendship is someone of the opposite sex, how do you keep a friendship from going beyond friendship? Two 16-year-olds, one from Minnesota and one from California, one a girl and one a boy, ask similar questions: "*Why is it that teenagers have to be 'going out' with someone always? I feel that I would rather just develop friendships with boys,*" and "*Why do kids think that everyone of the opposite sex has to be a 'girlfriend' or 'boyfriend'?*"

You need to have friends who are boys without having them called boyfriends or friends who are girls without having them called girlfriends. If you *want* the friendship to blossom out in other directions, that's OK too. But it should be your choice. There will come the day when your relationship with someone of the opposite sex will almost automatically take on a new flavor. You'll know when that day comes. In the meantime, friendships with both boys and girls set the stage for someday having a boyfriend or girlfriend—if you wish.

How do you get a chance to mix with others? How do you make contact with others so you can have or be a friend? Don't stay home! Get involved with activities at church and school. Volunteer. Join a club, even if you're not all that interested in what the club does. Dare to go to work on your school newspaper. Attend a dance and *dance*—especially you guys! When boys go to a dance and stand along the wall with their hands in their pockets, slouching and looking dumb, they really waste the evening—for themselves and for the girls who would like to dance with them.

More suggestions? Sure! Join a musical group. Try out for a school play even if you can't act. School plays never have enough set designers or makeup specialists or ticket sellers or prompters. Get involved. Every time you get involved in something, you will discover new potential friends. But you're not going to discover many friends hidden in your room behind your closed door! All you meet up there are your grumpy old thoughts and your twisted view of what the world is really like—and silence. Get out. Take the chance.

Are you taking a chance? Are there risks? You bet! You might be rejected, someone might say they don't like you, you might be passed by—all these are possible. But they're not very likely. What's more likely is that you will meet people who want to be cared for just like you do and who want to be wanted—by you. Move out toward life. You won't regret the effort.

More than friends

The most common question teenagers ask about friendships is this: "What about my relationship with a boyfriend (or girlfriend)?" A lot of young people feel like this young man who wrote, *The number one concern in my life is to develop a deep, meaningful, and lasting relationship with someone of the opposite sex.* I couldn't say it more clearly or directly. Many teenagers have that kind of yearning, but that kind of yearning can create problems, lots of problems.

Once when speaking to a group of teenagers, I made the point that you shouldn't "use" others. Here is the example of "using" I gave: A girl shouldn't accept an invitation to a dance from someone she really can't stand if all she wants to do is get to the dance. She would then be "using" that person. I believe that's wrong. I got this note back from the audience. *You said that if you're using somebody just to go to a dance that you should stay home. OK, so if somebody asks you to a dance that you really don't want to go with, but if you don't you won't get to go, you should say no. Well, what if somebody else asks you, after you said no to the other one, and you really like this person, what do you do because if you say yes you might hurt the first person?"*

Life is not easy when you get involved with other people! The only way out of that situation is by being very honest. Be honest from the beginning. Decline to go with the first person, but don't lie. That leaves you free to make the later choices you feel are necessary. See how it works?

It's obviously safer to have nothing to do with other people at all. Getting involved with other people can be a headache *("The thing that bothers me is my boyfriend,"),* just like *not* getting involved with other people can be a headache *("How come my sister can get a boyfriend and I can't?").* It's a risk. Involvement makes for tough situations. But the risk is worth taking, and the toughness is worth facing.

Listen to these concerns about boyfriends: *"The thing that's disturbing my life is trying to sort out my feelings about a guy." "How do you deal with competition or jealousy of my sex or opposite of my boyfriend?" "What do you do with jealous feelings when your ex-boyfriend starts going out with another girl? Do you pretend they aren't there or do you confess them to them?"*

Those three were "feeling" questions. They surface when all kinds of feelings are churning around inside you. One common feeling is jealousy. It's not a nice thing. It warps and it embitters and it leads you to do things you wouldn't otherwise do. The best thing to do with jealousy is to confront it. Why should you be miserable because another person is happy or has made a new discovery? Recognize jealousy (as did the young ladies who wrote the notes above) and get rid of it. Don't go around telling people you're jealous of them. If they already know it, they don't need you to tell them. If they don't know it, why trouble your relationship? Be more creative and constructive than that. Refuse to have any part of jealousy.

In addition to "feeling" questions, teenagers ask what I call "relationship" questions. Here are some examples:

1. *"What do you say to a guy when you like him and he doesn't like you?"*
2. *"What do you do if you like a guy and he doesn't like you?"*
3. *"What do you do if a guy likes you, but you don't like him? How do you tell him to 'get lost'?"*

4. *"What do you do when you like a guy and he likes someone else?"*
5. *"What do you do when you like a guy and he doesn't like you but he likes your best friend?"*
6. *"How do you tell a guy that you like him without getting both you and him embarrassed?"*

Just look at the subtle differences in these questions! Those differences make relationship questions exciting. For example, notice the difference between Questions 1 and 2. One asks what you *do* and the other asks what you *say*. Let's take *say* first. If he doesn't like you (I'm assuming that just means he doesn't feel toward you as intensely as you feel toward him—not that he despises you), there are a number of things to say. Say something pleasant like, "Hi! How are you?" Say something complimentary like, "That's a nice jacket!" Say something commendatory like, "You did all right at play practice!" Those are all *say* things. And there are a lot of them. They don't have to be earthshaking. Let your *say* be simple, truthful, and honest. You'd be surprised what simple, truthful, and honest statements do for developing relationships between people.

The *do* things are a bit trickier. Be very careful. Only do that which would be natural and normal, like helping with a class assignment or volunteering to do some project. *Do* smile. *Do* make yourself visible where he is, but not too conspicuous. You wouldn't want to smother him, would you? *Do* things both of you seem to like—like sing in a choir, attend a dance, or take a French course. But don't do anything you don't like to do, or wouldn't do, were you not trying to get his attention. Whenever you do those things, it shows, and they're not very effective.

Question 3 calls for honesty. If he isn't bugging you, don't do anything about him. Doing nothing is a message in itself. But if he's bothering you, tell him so in as pleasant a way as you can. Be very honest. Don't unnecessarily hurt him or make cutting remarks. Don't try a put-down. Be kind, but clear.

Questions 4 and 5 are very similar. It may be that you'll just have to harbor those feelings in your heart and go your way. Maybe he's not for you. If it's any comfort, there actually are an awful lot of nice guys in this world. There's no point in getting in a fight over any one. Try some of the things I suggested for Questions 1 and 2, and keep looking for another special guy. He's out there waiting for you.

The last question poses a problem that isn't really necessary to face. There's no reason you have to tell someone that you like him. It's usually rather obvious. If he likes you, it may work like this: One day when you're telling him you like something that he's doing, he will respond with a compliment for you. Then you might mention people you like and he seems to like. If the moment is right (and you'll know if it is), give a little laugh and say something like, "And I think you're OK too!" He can either laugh it off or react by getting a little more serious. Then see how it works out! Keep your relationship light until its gets heavy all by itself. But don't hurry—things move along fast enough by themselves. I've never forgotten the good advice of a father years ago when he encouraged his daughter to model her relationships with boys after the words on the mayonnaise jar: Keep cool but don't freeze.

There are many practical questions about boyfriending. A lot of them have to do with how you talk to boys, or how you talk in their company. *"What do you do when you just don't know how to say anything to a guy not knowing whether he's going to hate you or not after you've said it? In other words, if you're scared to talk about things in front of him?" "How can you get over being 'flustered' around guys?" "How do you let a guy know that you like him without feeling embarrassed? How do you find out if he likes you? Without asking right out?" "How can I talk honestly with my boyfriend?"*

We've had "feeling" questions and we've had "relationship" questions, and now here are some "talk" questions. They all have to do with the skills needed for sharing with another person. These are the same skills you need for talking with your parents or to a teacher or to a brother. In that sense, a boyfriend "talk" problem is no different. No matter with whom you are speaking, there are things you can do to make talking easier. Let me suggest a few.

Always look the person in the eye. Don't duck your head. Lift your chin and look them straight in the eye. *Smile.* Everyone is prettier when they smile. *Think about what you're going to say* for a moment. People won't think you're dumb if you're silent. *Encourage the other person to talk with you* by saying something like, "What do you think about that?" You'll soon discover folks like to have their advice solicited.

Give honest compliments. If someone has worked hard to look presentable, you know it. Say so. *Expect the best.* No one is going to abuse you or make fun of you. Be gently truthful and honest. Finally, *don't say negative things about others.* Always assume others will say *about* you *to* their friends what they say *to* you *about* their friends. It may not always be true, but it makes you watch your tongue.

Make a little checklist: eyes, chin, smile, think, question, compliment, honest. You won't go wrong. If you follow that sequence and he doesn't respond positively, then there's something wrong with him.

Here's a practical question girls face: *"How does a girl get a guy to dance?"* A lot of times the way to get a guy to dance is by teaching him how. Many guys don't know how! Teach him quietly. Don't embarrass him. Say something like, "I've learned a great new step. Let me teach you." Find a corner and go at it. In some places, it's OK to just ask a guy to dance. But that still turns a lot of guys off. Go slow. The best way to get to dance is by being fun to dance with. Be pleasant and caring for others. Send out positive vibrations. Even then, you might have a great evening, but still not dance! The truth is that boys are socially slower and a lot shyer than girls are. But a lot of them are reading this. Maybe they'll get a hint! Get an extra copy of this book and underline some things!

Here are two questions that will make you think: *"I recently broke up with my boyfriend and I feel I hurt him badly. How can I help him to understand I don't hate him, but just don't feel as close?"* and *"How do you break up with someone without hurting him too much?"*

I don't know of any painless way to break up a relationship. Just look at the words you use to describe what you're trying to do: *break up.* Wow! That's a bone-rattler. To break up means you're going to reverse the direction of a relationship, and that isn't easy. It's especially difficult to do without hurting the other person in any way.

It may be impossible. But you can make things easier and less painful.

Offer to return some of the gifts he gave you, like rings and personal mementos, that don't have the same kind of meaning now. Do it gently. I wouldn't offer to return articles of clothing, or things that have already been partly used. Don't do that unless you're asked to. Say the I-don't-hate-you words. Say the it's-been-a-wonderful-experience words too. That won't make it easier, but it surely doesn't make it any harder. Don't talk about the relationship you had with others. Let what happened be just between the two of you. No one likes to hear thirdhand reports about personal things. It will still hurt, but if you handle the matter this way, the experience will be a little less painful. Meanwhile, get on with living. You will survive.

One more practical question: *"What should you do when there's a person that you don't like but on your birthday they're always right there giving you a gift?"* That's a tough one. That's like the question about discouraging unwanted relationships. The only solution I can think of is honesty. But let the honesty be proportionate to the gift. You can gently laugh at a modest memento or some small or inexpensive expression of caring you receive without hurting the person. But if it's a larger gift, you must be ready to say in as kind a way as you can, "I can't accept this gift from you. We don't know each other well enough, and I would feel like I am using you." When the writer says the giver is someone she doesn't like, she is probably referring to someone who has feelings of affection for her that she doesn't reciprocate in kind. The I-like-you-like-a-brother explanation is a bit tough on the male pride, but it's often the most honest thing you can say. In any event, you must not accept a gift when acceptance insinuates a different message from the one you want to send.

Now let's turn to the other side of the coin: girlfriends. I've always liked the honesty of the teenage boy who wrote: *"If I live to be a hundred, I'll never understand about women."* I think he'd just gone through a bad time! But do people ever react when I share his words!

Does this one surprise you? *"I just moved and at the new place the girls are very aggressive and I have been asked out by them and it drives me nuts."* I get a lot of notes like that. Does it make you think? Or how about this cryptic message from an Eastern teenager: *"My biggest problem is no girlfriend."*

The questions boys ask are different from questions girls ask. Actually, almost all the questions boys ask have to do with one subject: "How do I talk with girls?" They mean just exactly what they say. They want to know how they can send a clear verbal message to somebody so that that special person can understand what they're trying to say. Isn't that what these four notes mean? *"How do you tell someone you care for them very much (maybe even love)?" "My biggest problem is talking to girls." "The thing most bothering me is a girl that I date but I don't know how to tell her how much I really like her." "The thing most bothering me right now is my relationship to a girl. I do not know exactly how to act or how much she likes me, but I like her."* How do you get conversations going under those circumstances? How do you let someone else know how you feel?

It may sound old-fashioned, but if we want to communicate, we all need to learn more about what used to be called "the social graces." The social graces include politeness, how to give a compliment, how to be comfortable and make others comfortable at a dinner or dance, how to act in a caring fashion toward others. None of those are easily developed skills. They require a conscious effort and commitment. But a polite person stands out! You will discover when you are polite people hear you more clearly, and you will find it easier to speak with them.

Another suggestion is to read a book about how people think and feel or talk with someone who can help you understand things like that. This book is an example of the kind of book I mean, and there are many more. Probably the best "book" to review is the one that you write within your own mind. That book is written as you watch the world in which you live, and recognize in that world those things which make sharing easier, like lifting your chin and looking people in the eye.

Here's another suggestion: Find a subject you know your friend would like to talk about. Find one where she (or he) is competent and skilled and talk to their strength. That way at least one person in the conversation

will be at ease. When your conversational partner is at ease, you'll find you're more at ease too. Give a genuine compliment, ask for an opinion—these will help the conversational process.

After introductory conversational preparations such as these, you are on your way to talking about more personal matters. Actual serious conversation may happen weeks or months after you have first met your friend, but when that moment arrives, the conversation will flow with more casual naturalness. Take your time. A blundering hurriedness invariably ends up embarrassing either you or your friend. The only thing worse than conversational "shoving" is trying to send a message by silence. No one knows what silence means! It's no message. The only thing you can do with silence is suffer. So learn how to send clear messages. Learn how to send them well. Learn how to send them in ways that make others comfortable. You can develop those skills.

Behind these two questions: *How do you ask a girl to dance?* and *I would like advice about not being scared to kiss my girlfriend,* is hidden the same old bugaboo—fear of rejection. Both guys are wondering how to deal with it.

Let me emphasize something I've said before: *It hurts to be rejected, it really hurts.* No one wants to be rejected. But there's another part to the message: *You will survive.* You can live through rejection. So go ahead and take risks, but risk with increasing carefulness. Learn how to "read" other people and how to be sensitive to what might be potential rejection areas. If you try a clumsy, abrupt, pushy smooch on your first date, I wouldn't be a bit surprised if you are rejected. You deserve it. Don't do that. Take your time. Go slow. Let the circumstance set the pace. Practice the communication skills we've been talking about. Learn those things that make sharing easier and caring simpler. As you do, the risk of rejection diminishes.

You won't develop those skills overnight. That's one of the reasons God gave you so many teenage years. Use those years carefully. Even though you won't learn all the important communication things overnight, you will learn them if you just keep plugging away. Then people will say about you, "I wish I had the same natural ability for dealing with others that you do." Inside yourself, you'll just laugh. They'll never know how long you worked and how hard you tried to make it look so easy. The effort pays off.

Before I close this chapter on friendship, let's talk about love and marriage. Friendships have a way of growing and drawing couples closer and closer until the relationship intensifies into what we call love. Love? What is love? How would you answer that question?

Love is a funny word. The dictionary doesn't really define it. Literature doesn't define it. But the dictionary and literature and conversation *describe how love acts.* We recognize whether or not love is present by actions. That's what St. Paul said when he gave us the wonderful description of love in 1 Corinthians 13. Just look at all the ways love acts that he lists in those few verses.

Because love is so hard to define, we need to be very careful when looking at love. It's too important a subject for us to be confused about it. We need to be very careful especially when our feelings of love could possibly lead to another important step in human relations: marriage. To highlight the concern, let me share a few of the love-and-marriage questions that I've received.

"Do you think that a 16-year-old girl can really be in love?" Of course. I believe you can honestly and fully fall in love at any age. But you can also be infatuated or starry-eyed and confused at any age. Look at all the adults who thought they were in love enough to get married, and then saw their relationship destroyed in divorce. Age isn't the only important thing to consider. I believe teenage love can be every bit as intense and serious and real as love at any other stage of life.

But love is never an excuse for doing something dumb or irresponsible or sudden. Love should make you more sensitive to the consequences of your actions, and to the intelligent acceptance of those consequences. It should make you be more care-full (that is, "full of care"). Love should make you so caring about other people that you wouldn't think of doing anything to, or with, them that might compromise them or bring them hurt or make life more difficult for them.

I think teenage love is real and possible. My heart goes out to the 15-year-old who wrote, *"Both my parents are upset about my relationship with my girlfriend—saying I* can't love her." Maybe in their judgment he *doesn't* love her, and maybe in their opinion he *shouldn't* love her, but that's got nothing to do with whether or not he *can* love her.

True love doesn't offer silly arguments. Listen to this: *"How do you break it to your parents that you're engaged? Times have changed around our town and kids are getting married at a younger age—my parents don't realize this."* That's a dumb question and dumber statement. There are many better reasons for being engaged and getting married than "times have changed around our town and kids are getting married at a younger age." More than that, if someone is engaged and still hasn't told the parents involved, that's irresponsible. If you can't start out on the up and up with your mom and dad, you'll never make it through life with your partner when things get tough. If you can't face your parents or your partner's parents, you'll never make it successfully with each other. I would respond to that question with another question: "How do you break it to a 17-year-old that she isn't anywhere near ready to be engaged if she hasn't figured out a way to discuss a matter that important with her parents?" Marriage is much too serious a matter to back into or to feel it's something you have to do.

Here are four more love-and-marriage questions—two of each.

1. *"How do you know you're really in love?"*
2. *"How can you tell you are in love? What is a good, pliable definition of love in all senses, physical and mental?"*
3. *"How can you tell you are in love with a guy enough to marry him? For marriage for good?"*
4. *"What things will let me know when I finally find the perfect marriage partner—will I hear bells? See angels, etc.?"*

One surefire sign you are in love is that you feel like you are in love. If you don't understand what I mean by that, then one thing is sure: You aren't in love. And love is more than being sexually aroused by your partner. Sexuality may not even play a significant part early in your emotional relationship.

Here is a checklist that you should go through which can help you determine if you're in love.

1) You should like the person with whom you think you're in love. Do you?
2) You should be proud to be with him or her and happy to introduce him or her to your family and your friends. Are you?
3) The two of you ought to have similar feelings about many things, holding a number of opinions in common. Is that true?
4) Neither of you should make all the decisions or dominate the relationship. How does that work out in your situation?
5) No one should play a game called if-you-loved-me-you-would _____ (you fill in the blank). Have you played that game?
6) You should feel good about your relationship and positive about continuing it. Do you?

If you can answer those questions in the right way (and you know what the right way is), then I think you're in love. But not all love results in marriage.

After love, marriage is a good option when:
1) Both people want it.
2) Neither is in the process of rebounding from another relationship with someone else.
3) Both can carry their responsible share of the family emotional, intellectual, and spiritual needs.
4) You have enough money to live on.
5) You know how to forgive and be forgiven.
6) Your family and friends support your decision.

Other things could be listed. For instance, it makes marriage so much easier when the husband and wife share a common commitment of faith in Jesus Christ; when they've known each other long enough to understand the basic areas of potential disagreement; when neither intellectually or emotionally dominates the other. But that premarriage checklist of six items is an awfully good place to begin. If you work your way through those six points (and your own additions), you'll know whether you should seriously consider marriage and how soon it ought to happen.

All my comments in the love-and-marriage section so far are built on the assumption that you've got someone to love or marry. What about these two very real concerns: *"When will God send me someone who will love me and who I can love?"* and *"Will I ever find the right girl to share my life with in marriage?"*

I don't know the specific answer to those two questions. I don't know when God will send you someone to love and be loved by. But ask him to do just that. Then busy yourself at the task of becoming lovable. Develop those traits which draw others to you—traits like positiveness, good manners, gentleness, caring, Christian conduct. If you develop those approaches to living, two things will take place.

First, you won't need to put any relationship on a "must" list in your life. You will be so well put together by the grace of God you won't worry about incidental questions. Second, you will make yourself so charming that friends will come at you from every direction. The best way to attract friends (and what finer basic relationship for marriage could there be?) is by being a friend.

Warm up all those friendly skills and get busy with the business of building some great relationships. When you've learned how to have and be a friend, then the song "What a Friend We Have in Jesus" will take on a newer and broader and more powerful meaning. What a friend *he* is! He was our friend first and teaches us how to be really friendly.

SIX

Getting Along
with Your Sexual Feelings

I get a lot of questions about the meaning of sex and the practice of sexual relations. It's interesting to me that I've never had a question about how to engage in sexual relations. Most teenagers know that scene pretty well. They know the minimum mechanics. They get their questions answered in classrooms at school or in conversation with others or in books they read. Some of their information is wrong, some of it is right. But the mystery of the meaning and impact of sexual relations and the understanding of how sex can be abused—these subjects keep coming up for discussion all the time. And with them come questions like these.

"If a guy you like a lot and are kind of going with turns around, right after you've seen him, goes and makes out with another girl, what kind of relationship should there be? What I did was just forget him and look for some other guy. Is this right? If not, what should I do? He's constantly talking to me at school. He also said he was sorry for that night. But he could do it again." *"How many guys want to marry a virgin?"* *"My mother has difficulty in letting me date. Times have changed since my sister was there. Just because she made a mistake doesn't mean that I will."* *"Why do people use sex to play with?"* *"I'm concerned with my life and the things I've done through sex—I just ask forgiveness."*

When I review all the questions I have received about sexual relations, I find they fall into three broad categories. First there are questions about *how far* a person should go in relating to another person sexually. Then there is a group of questions that ask *what's wrong with* . . . ? Finally there are the *curiosity questions;* questions of concern or interest.

How far should I . . . ?

Kids usually ask their most important question right up front: *"How far should I go on my first date?"* What do you think?

The answer to that question starts with the recognition that sexually and physically teenagers are men and women. Some mature earlier than others, but from the earliest days of the teenage years, almost all are fully capable of a complete sexual response to sexual stimulations. Over the years their understanding of sexuality will grow. Eventually most will marry and will give proper expression to their affection for their marriage partner through sexual relations. Others won't wait to be bound to marriage. They want sexual relations now. They are wrong. The Christian view of sex places full sexual expression within the boundaries of marriage. Not before. *Full* sexual expression belongs within marriage.

Now let's start with that first question. The question was, *"How far should I go on my first date?"* I wouldn't go anywhere. Why should you? You have no obligation to be sexually responsive to a person whom you are just trying to discover. If your character, personality, and appearance are not attractive enough for him or her, then don't muddy the waters by playing around with sexual things. Keep the earliest relationships light—very light. Necking or petting or any kind of sensual caressing is out of place on the first date. Start out with a handshake. A lot of great lifelong love affairs began that way. If he or she doesn't find that sufficient, then he or she won't be too impressed with the rest of your Christian character either! Don't be pressed into doing anything that leaves you uncomfortable. And don't buy into dippy sensuality. It's a drag.

Here's another common question: *"How far should a*

'good girl' go with a guy?" That question works for "good guys" too! The answer? Not very far down the sexual road.

The Bible says, "Avoid the passions of youth" (2 Tim. 2:22). That passage means you shouldn't play with sexual fire. It also means don't play near sexual fire. It also means don't try to determine how close you can stand to the sexual fire before you're scorched! A more important concern is the other person—who he or she is and where you are going. When you are sexually aroused or are sexually arousing someone else, both of you know it. Don't act dumb. Sex is not for dumb people—and it's no toy! Back off whenever the expectations you are developing in yourself (or someone else) are more than the fulfillment you know you should be offering or accepting. Understand? Read it again. Included in that answer is consideration for the intensity of your relationship, consideration for your emotional condition, and consideration for your friend. All three are important. You're never going to get a road map to follow on the highway of sexuality. But long before you've gone too far, you know where you're heading. Apply brakes. Put it in reverse. He (or she) will love you for it.

What happens if you and your companion are ready for the world of marriage and are interested in uniting for life? What about these questions: *What does the Bible say about premarital sex?" "How far can you go before you get married?" "Where does the Bible say that it is a sin or wrong to be intimate before marriage?"*

Scripture makes it very clear that one of the reasons for marriage is the satisfaction of our fundamental (and God-given) human sexual hungers and needs. St. Paul said it so clearly: "It is better to marry than to burn" (1 Cor. 7:9). It really is! Realizing that God has established marriage as the context in which sexual relations should take place, it's clear in Scripture that the sexual sequence should be (a) *marriage* and (b) *sexual relations*. Whenever you get *a* and *b* inverted, you are in trouble. And when there is no *a* even considered with *b,* then you're dealing with flat-out sin. You are either using or being used—or both. The words that condemn this kind of activity (depending upon your sexual partner) are the biblical words *fornication* and *adultery*. The biblical view is that one man and one woman, committed to each other in marriage, are permitted and encouraged to have sexual relations. It's a God-given privilege, not a right!

Oops! I'm getting ahead of myself in answers. Let's listen to some more questions first.

What's wrong with . . . ?

I call these "What's wrong with . . . ?" questions. *"What do you say to a couple who feel they are honestly in love and have genuine concern for one another about premarital sex?" "Before marriage: how far can (should) two people go and still be right in God's eyes?"*

Questions about sexual relations between two people who intend to get married and who then do get married are different from questions about sexual relations between young people who don't. The answers I'm about to give are directed to a couple who will get married to each other (and I would add soon), and who are struggling within themselves with questions about premarital sex.

I can't find in the Bible a specific statement about premarital relations between a couple who will soon be married. As a matter of fact, the Bible seems to suggest that when a couple has committed themselves to one another, they are as married as they will ever get! But there are some strong hints about the caring way marriage and sex should be seen and practiced by young people who are about to commit themselves, for life, to one another. And it's very clear that there are strong and absolutely crystal-clear statements that have to do with adultery (breaking an existing marriage covenant) and sexual promiscuousness (having sexual relations with a number of people—or even one—with no clear intention of ultimate marriage). In those instances, sexual intercourse is called a sin, and the judgment of God is upon it. It brings no joy or peace to anyone.

But when the argument goes like this, "Why should we wait in our sexual relationship to each other since we love one another now and will soon be married anyway?" then the situation is a little different. My strongest encouragement for you is, "Wait anyway." There are good reasons.

94

No matter how serious your intentions, not every intense and loving commitment ends in marriage. Things happen to hinder that goal. Don't further confuse what will probably become a very complicated issue under the best of circumstances by having to wonder whether your sexual relations was what actually committed you to each other.

There will be times in your marriage when you will wonder if you married the right person. That question comes to every relationship. If you have premarital sexual relations, it will be more difficult to develop a clear answer to that question. You may end up wondering, "Would I have married him (or her) if we hadn't had sexual relations before our marriage?"

Further, there's a very thin line between wanting to share a sexual oneness and the need to "use" someone sexually. Your understanding of that line and your serious caring about that line is sharper if, before your sexual relationship begins, you've already made a public and lifelong commitment to each other.

But I also want to encourage you to make very sure that you aren't just testing each other arbitrarily. If there's no good reason for you to wait with your marrying until next June—or a year from now—don't do it. Don't pick arbitrary dates a long time in the distance. That will end up testing you unnecessarily! Get married as soon as you can. Once you know that's what you want to do, and you're in a position to do it, start the wedding march! Don't tease yourself, or someone else, with no cause. And don't let your parents' ideas about when and where and how you should get married color the decision you know ought to be made.

Having said that, I need to make one other extremely important point: You aren't ready to get married until you're ready to get married. Read it again. Here's what I mean.

Young *love* is great. But young *marriages* are awesome and frightening. They break down at a rapid rate. The reasons include these:

1) Young married people are still developing and they change during their first years of marriage. Those changes make it easy for them to grow apart.

2) There's not enough money to maintain a household

in the way the couple wants. That makes for more frustration and anger than can be handled.

3) There hasn't been enough social preparation. You can be in love in your teens, but you're smart if you don't get married until much later! Get an education—first. Begin a career of some sort—first. Save money—first. Make sure you're really grown up and have set the mold that you're going to follow—first.

That's not foolish advice. And, although you know yourself best, most couples are very smart if they wait until their latest teens or early twenties before they get married. Don't move too quickly!

I've been wondering about . . .

Here is a series of questions from kids. They are not directly connected to each other, but they all deal with common concerns teenagers have about sexual relationships.

1) *"Why does a girl get a bad reputation if she does it but a guy doesn't?"*

I don't know. I know it's often true. But I'm really not sure that a guy doesn't get some kind of strange reputation for his sexual casualness as well. There are a lot of girls who won't date guys with smoky histories. One thing is for sure—knowing this is true ought to give you some idea of how even the world understands and evaluates sexual promiscuousness. It's no honor!

2) *"What about sex before marriage? What if that strong one-to-one love that exists in a marriage is there before the actual marriage?"*

If it's there before marriage, then get married. That's one of the tests of marital readiness. But "playing house" is not the same as *building a house*. If you're ready to get married, get married. By the same token, if you're not ready to get married, don't. Here's the sequence: First love; then marriage.

3) *"What is wrong with living with a guy before you are married?"*

What's wrong is that it's sin—and it's dumb. The sin part is clear. The dumb part is becoming more clear. Couples who live together say they are trying to find out whether or not they are compatible and then might get married. Studies now show that the incidence of divorce is higher among couples who have lived together before marriage than those who haven't, so that argument is shot. Living together is no insurance against divorce, nor is it a guaranteed aid for a good marriage. God's idea of living together is when two people who have a common commitment toward each other have publicly stated their commitment and are ready to practice that commitment through whatever years yet remain in either one's life. It's also called marriage.

4) *"How far should my boyfriend and I go? We've never had sex, but we've gone fairly far (oral sex) and I feel guilty, but I know he wants it (he won't bother me about it—never) and I don't want to hurt him because I love him."*

I don't know what all those words mean, but they sound very slippery and the reasoning they offer is strange and suspicious. Basically, I would say that you shouldn't do anything that ends up with you feeling guilty. That should tell you you are wrong! And you shouldn't do anything about which you end up feeling guilty because you think someone "wants" you to do it. Great human tragedies develop from the kind of strange reasoning that filters through this whole question. It sounds to me like the young lady involved is doing what she wants to do and is using her boyfriend's "wants" as an excuse. It won't work.

5) *"If a couple has chosen to know each other through intercourse, should they therefore feel bound to stay together? How can they start over feeling good if they separate?"*

They can't start over feeling good. There's nothing to feel good about. What they did was wrong. They can be forgiven, but they can't change what happened. The thing to do is confess your sins before God and change your ways. This note sounds very calculated to me. If someone has "chosen" to do something, it was no accident. Before God, they should stay together. If they don't, it's just plain old sin.

6) *"If you have sexual relations with someone when you are not married, what kind of 'hurt' does it bring your parents?"*

The hurt it brings to your parents is the same hurt a

parent feels any time their child does something that brings pain to the child's life. It's the same hurt that God the Father feels when we, his children, sin. Parents hate to see their children do the kinds of things that won't bring them peace and happiness but will bring, instead, heartache and sadness. But that's still not the reason to keep yourself sexually clean. Do it for yourself.

7) *"How do you know that he or she is (not) 'that type'?"*

You don't. Everyone is "that type." We are all potentially capable of doing anything. St. Paul said, "I know that good does not live in me—that is, in my human nature" (Rom. 7:18). Don't tease yourself thinking you are above temptation. You aren't. Don't tease others. They aren't beyond temptation either.

8) *"How can you tell if a guy is a 'lech' or not?"*

Easy. Look at him. Check his actions. Listen to his words. You'll know quickly enough. The same goes for girls. But be sure you do the looking *first*. There's nothing Christian about being gullible in your relationships with other people. You've got the right and responsibility to check people out.

9) *"When 'sex' (the subject) comes up in the family, it is always dismissed as 'dirty.' Why in this time and age?"*

I don't know. I don't know what can be done to educate people about the need for honest conversation on the subject of sex. I could list some reasons why people might be reluctant to share, but then I would only be guessing. I do know that it's bad when healthy Christian conversations on this important item never take place. Whether you can "train" your mother or dad to change is one question. But you can train yourself. Make sure, when you are a mother or father, that open sharing on the subject of sex happens between you and your children.

10) *"What age is a good age for starting dating? How does one handle the temptation of premarital sex?"*

Start dating whenever it's natural. For most young people, that seems to surface somewhere between the ages of 15 and 18. It can be forced earlier, but when that happens it's usually gawky and strained. But don't be depressed if you neither have a date, nor a desire to date, until you're well past 18. That's OK. I'm convinced

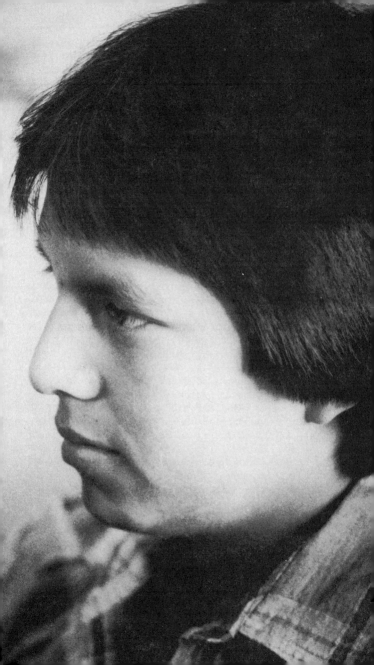

that there are many, many more who first date after 18 than there are who date before 16. Check it out. And the best way to deal with any kind of temptation, no matter what its character, is by prayer and by avoiding the source of the problem. Don't hang around where temptations hover. Make yourself scarce.

What happens when, against all this good advice, a Christian fails? For one thing, we bring pain into our lives and the lives of others. But God has a good word for us even then. Never forget that. His good word is that in Christ there is forgiveness. I'd like to share this note that was handed me at a youth gathering by a young lady. Listen to what she has to say.

"I'd like for you to emphasize that God forgives us if we come to him no matter what our sin. When I was a sophomore in college, I 'gave' my virginity under some pressure to a guy I didn't really respect but thought I loved. After lasting so long through high school and early college, I was crushed the next day. I felt dirty, ashamed, and scared. Worst of all, I felt that because I had lost my virginity, I had lost it all. There is so much emphasis on it and I knew that it couldn't be replaced. Feeling that way, I figured that there was now no choice for me. I was a 'bad' girl so I should act that way. Well, I didn't feel good enough about myself to talk to anyone about it. It's taken a long time to learn to love myself again. I was lucky. I met a wonderful man and told him everything thinking he couldn't possibly want me. Instead, he loved me and helped me grow back into God's family. I'm very happy now, married, with a son. Please share with girls that nothing is unforgivable and that God and his family will love them anyway. They have a choice."

I think that's a great letter for girls—and for boys—and for folks of every age.

SEVEN

Getting Along
with God and His Church

Are teenagers religious? You'd better believe it! They have a passion and a commitment to the Lord and his church that is exciting and pleasant to behold. This is true even though they have a lot of questions about things religious for which they don't get many good answers.

I offer that observation for three reasons. First, I have spent most of my adult life working in a close relationship with teenagers. I was and am a pastor. I was and am *their* pastor. I have "pastored" thousands of young people. I've taught them. I've listened to their hurts. I've sensed their pains. I've tried to answer their questions. I've seen them wrestle with the age-old spiritual conundrums as each new generation discovers them. I've heard them state what they believe. I've watched them live their lives. Some would expect me to say they are no more religious or Christian than any other age, but I don't believe that. My conclusions, from observation, are that they want to be, and often are, considerably more religious than most previous generations in modern history.

The second reason supporting my conclusions is the accumulated experience I've gained speaking before thousands of young people in large and small gatherings, usually in surroundings other than a church. I've watched them in hotels as they've gone from religious class to religious class all day long. Many times I thought they had every right, and considerable reason, to lie back and relax. They didn't. The subjects under discussion were always carefully prepared with an eye toward teenage concerns, but it takes more than a slick title to lure hundreds of young people into a crowded room for more than an hour while things religious are presented. They hunger and thirst.

The third reason for my opinion is the notes I receive and the mail that regularly plops into my box. So many of the questions and so much of teenagers' concern has to do with God, with his church, and with religion. The church is generally an unstated but assumed aspect of teenagers' religious questions. The kids I hear from are basically churched. They have had considerable religious training. The question is whether they'll continue to be churched when they leave their teens and go on into their 20s. Time will tell. For now I believe the ones who come to these gatherings and participate in the religious activities (and don't forget for a moment that this totals hundreds of thousands of young people) have a solid and significant link to the church.

Well, what kind of questions do they ask? Here's one from a 15-year-old boy from Charlotte: *"I don't have quite all the information on the Lord I need to know."* A 16-year-old stated, *"The thing that is disturbing my life is that I am not acting as a total Christian."* How's this for a teenage question? *"How (or if) can I discern with any degree of certainty (which my humanity permits) what things (guidance, ideas, feelings) come from the Spirit in my everyday life as opposed to the things which come from my own selfish sinfulness or Satan? If there is no way it seems to me that I am in darkness and unable to follow the will of my Father."* That's a powerful question! It is "religious" to the core and it is typical in tone if not in content. Let me share more.

A 16-year-old asked, *"I have a 15-year-old friend who recently became paralyzed from the neck down from an accident. She will never walk again. How can God's love allow such a thing or how can God's love be made real in her life to keep her going?"* And a younger lady (age 14) wanted to know, *"What age do you think a person should be baptized?"* Both of those inquiries are incredibly deep and are serious religious questions. They move in the areas great philosophers and religious thinkers of the centuries have studied. The 14-year-old needs a Nicodemus-like discussion from John 3. The 16-year-old would be blessed by a chat with, and about, Job or about the crucifixion or about Psalm 23. But all that sharing best takes place face-to-face, faith-to-faith, and eye-to-eye. For right now, recognize that those common teenage questions are extremely caring and sensitive.

There are a lot more concerns—let me share just two more. The first is from a 19-year-old guy and the second from a 15-year-old girl. *"I'm trying to live a fulfilling (fun) life as a Christian when the whole world appears evil, and I'm trying to figure out where I fit in the Lord's plan." "My problem is knowing what God wants me to do with my life."* These are just some examples of the incredibly deep and searching probings toward life that flow out of the hearts and from the pens of teenage Christians.

Lest I leave you with the impression that everyone under 20 is a theological whiz and a budding Martin Luther, I also receive a lot of questions like this: *"Are there really pearly gates?"* The answer? I don't know whether there are gates made of pearls in heaven or not, but there *is* a place in God's universe where we will all meet the real pearl of great price, Jesus Christ, our Savior. When we meet him, I don't think we're going to be concerned with the construction or material content of any gate that happens to be standing around.

The religious questions I receive from young people fall into the same categories as the chapters of this book: questions about themselves, questions about parents, general family questions, and questions about friends. Could it be that teenagers (or maybe all of us) live "square" lives bound by those four borders of concern?

Personal religion and personal faith

There's no question more basic to the religious stability of people than this one: *"I'd like to challenge and question my faith and Christianity, to learn more about it, but I'm afraid I won't find satisfactory answers and will thus lose it. Help!"*

Of course you should challenge and question your faith! If it *is* a faith—a real faith—it will stand. If it collapses under the pressure of a curious fundamental probing, then you really haven't lost much. There wasn't any substance to it anyway. It's better to begin with a bare bones basic foundation of faith that can take pressure than try to maintain a bulky and highly decorative religious superstructure that has no content. Begin with a simple foundation statement and build a *real* religion from there. Here are some examples of how to do just that.

Is there anything more elementary than the earliest Christian statement of faith "Jesus is Lord"? That's the place to begin—with the lordship of Christ. Move from there to the first gathered statement about what Christians hold dear: the Apostles' Creed. It's about as basic as you can get. Move on from there to the Nicene Creed, followed by carefully working through something like *Luther's Small Catechism*. That little book is a jewel. Once you're through memorizing the answers and start really reading them, you'll realize how carefully each phrase is attached to the next and how packed with meaning each paragraph can be.

And the Bible? Of course. These other aids will lead you to and through the Bible. That's what St. Paul talks about in 2 Tim. 3:14-17. Dig around right now and find that specific portion of Scripture. Listen to what Paul has to say, not only to Timothy, but to all of us. Ask all kinds of questions. Ask them eagerly. But always be prepared for the kind of answers that are coming to you out of his Word and the walk of faith toward which he encourages you. Don't be afraid.

Don't forget who gives faith—your faith included! Remember the passage, "No one can confess 'Jesus is Lord,' unless he is guided by the Holy Spirit" (1 Cor. 12:3). That statement of Scripture is what the Small Catechism teaches in the Third Article of the Apostles' Creed. Recall the words with me, and if you've never seen it before, now's a good time to meet this great statement of faith: "I believe that I cannot by my own understanding or effort believe in Jesus Christ my Lord, or come to him. But the Holy Spirit has called me through the Gospel, enlightened me with his gifts, and sanctified and kept me in true faith. In the same way he calls, gathers, enlightens, and sanctifies the whole Christian church on earth, and keeps it united with Jesus Christ in the one true faith."

Not everything that teenagers say is affirming and encouraging. How about this: *"I'm concerned with the things I'm getting out of my Christianity—and the things that are not interesting to me about my church."* I'm concerned too. This young man needs to know that many things about the church don't "interest" a lot of people. While the church is God's idea, its daily care and upkeep is in the hands of people. People who handle the church sometimes do it with a tenderness that is beautiful. Others are rude and crude and overbearing and bring shame to the church. But no matter whether it be loving hands or brutal hands, the church is Christ's bride (Ephesians 5). The picture of the church as the bride of Christ is quite lovely, even when the bride gets battered. When she is battered, it's not his work, but ours.

If you find you have trouble getting interested in church, you need to be reminded how the process works. When you don't invest anything, you don't get any interest. That's the way it is in the banking world, and that's the way it is in the church world as well. Invest yourself in the church and just see what you get! You'll be surprised—and blessed! Care for the church with the intensity Christ cared for you. If we all did that, God's assembly of his children gathered in churches would give off an overwhelmingly attractive brightness! Didn't he say, "Your light must shine before people, so that they will see the good things you do and praise your Father in heaven"? (Matt. 5:16). You'd better believe he did! He needs more followers burning brightly. Brightly burning Christians make for an "interesting" church.

Here are three more personal statements from teenagers who put their finger on one of the great problems of living with a faith. *"I believe in God, but I guess my parents haven't ever made me go regularly to church, so now I don't go except on special occasions. After I do go I know within myself I feel so good. Is it wrong to be happy with the kind of worship you do and with the relationship you have with God, when you know you could do it more often? How or what can I do to get my parents to go with me?"* *"I don't feel I'm close enough to Christ. I don't feel like a Christian."* *"I don't feel as close to Christ as I would like and I would like to change it."* That kind of "feeling" question can be dangerous—here's why.

God's revealed facts are more dependable than feelings. As a matter of fact, feelings can confuse his facts. You can "feel" good when you're really quite ill, and you can "feel" bad without being seriously sick at all. Feelings, whether positive or negative, are not a dependable guide in the Christian life. Feelings can and do deceive. I'm a Christian not because I *feel* like I'm one, but because it's a fact Christ made me one. That fact is clearly underwritten and proven by his crucifixion on Calvary. I am close to Christ not because I *feel* near him, but because he walks with me and will not let me go. He will not separate himself from me. Just listen to this: "Who, then, can separate us from the love of Christ? Can trouble do it, or hardship or persecution or hunger or poverty or danger or death? . . . No, in all these things we have complete victory through him who loved us! For I am certain that nothing can separate us from his love: neither death nor life, neither angels nor other heavenly rulers or powers, neither the present nor the future, neither the world above nor the world below—there is nothing in all creation that will ever be able to separate us from the love of God which is ours through Christ Jesus our Lord" (Rom. 8:35-39).

That great truth of Christianity is *not* based on my feelings. It is based on fact—God's fact. Hang in there when you really don't feel good about your faith. Your feelings won't influence the fact that God doesn't quit where you're concerned. Every major character in Scripture had times when he didn't feel right about what he was doing or how he was acting. I'm speaking about great people like Moses, Peter, Mary, and Martha, just to name a few. Check them out. Read the Bible and see the facts of God's love shown. Find strength for your convictions by going to places where the Bible is regularly read and studied, where many friends in Christ are actively building up each other through the facts of our faith! If you ever need to choose between the facts of faith and your feelings, go with the facts every time!

Here are two other typical "feeling" questions and comments by teenagers. The first writer was about to take the big step out of the teens and on to 20. *"How can a person as a Christian discover joy and hope? I've been brought up in the church and have always considered myself a*

Christian, but for the last four years have been very unhappy and even considering suicide. I know that hell is bad and that I'm wrong to feel this way, but lately even though I try I can't feel happy about anything and am very depressed." Did you see those "feels" in there? A 15-year-old wrote: "Why is it that a person who says she is a Christian has so many doubts about God? I believe in Jesus Christ, but I find it hard to believe there is a Father such as God on whom our/my faith and life is based." Her trouble is with the facts.

The devil uses doubt to destroy joy and hope and undercut faith. He doesn't want you to know that there's always a tension between believing and not believing; between conviction and confusion; between faith and doubt. We read in Scripture this statement: "I do have faith, but not enough. Help me have more!" (Mark 9:24). On the greatest believing days there are still moments and times of doubt. Because of this tension from Satan, we need other people to help us. We are told in Scripture that we are supposed to encourage one another with "psalms, hymns, and sacred songs" (Col. 3:16). How can we support one another if we aren't together? Christian togetherness helps fight doubt. Don't get separated from the church, off by yourself. Stick together with all the people of God. We all need the reinforcing presence of others to help us remember again and again all the facts God has left for us. Otherwise we are stuck with our feelings. Members of Christian communities everywhere build up one another. Find one of those communities. Hook yourself to it. Get involved. Don't try to go it alone—live arm in arm with brothers and sisters in Christ.

Look out for weird cults that prey on lonely young people. They can suck you in, fill your heads with strange statements, and use you for their own purposes. Avoid people users. Get with proven Christians!

My family and my faith

Want to hear a typical disconnected comment about religion, faith, and a teenager's family? Here's one from a 17-year-old Minnesota teenager: "My brother and sister-in-law have gone through some real bad marital troubles though things are getting better. My mother resigned from *the church and she goes to another one. I go to our Lutheran church and father stays home to watch Dr. Schuller on TV. Mom and Dad have marital difficulties in excess."*

There wasn't much missing in that note, was there? Sounds like the scenario for a soap opera! Parental conflict. Marital discord. Electronic religion. Split family worship. In-law tension. Other than that, things are OK. Is that disconnected but sensitive sentence normal? Yes, it is! That sentence is a wedge of the "real life" everyone tells teenagers to get ready for. But teenagers don't have time to get ready for it—they're already in it!

Here are some comments from kids about practical churchy things and home: *"My parents don't like to haul me around to church. They don't like activities all the time. There's too much running around all the time, too far to go." "My last problem is that I went away last weekend on a retreat and this weekend I told them I was going away again and they called me a religious freak and say that I spend too much time at church. What do I do?"*

Can you believe that parents get upset with kids who want to be more deeply involved in religion, with the church, and with other young people? There are a lot of teenagers who get absolutely no help from home! Instead they get hassled. When you see people who are caught in a bind like that, help them out. Give them a ride or support and encourage them.

How about this question: *"My father is not a Christian. He was 'religioned' to death when he was a kid. I haven't been able to find a good approach in witnessing to him. Why is it so difficult to witness to members of your own family?"*

While I've met a lot of people who talked about being "religioned to death" as a child, I really haven't run into anyone for whom that statement was supported by fact. It makes a great excuse, but usually it's just a lot of baloney. The best way to witness to that father is to talk to him about his real Father, and his brother, Jesus. That brother is the only one truly "religioned to death." Introduce them to each other by tender and caring actions and gentle words. Witnessing in the family is very difficult for most of us because there are so many inconsistencies between our words and our actions. People at home see those inconsistencies most clearly.

108

A man of words and not of deeds
Is like a garden full of weeds.

Do you understand that little rhyme? It calls all of us to fill our garden with the plants that produce the fruits of the Spirit like those Paul lists in Gal. 5:22-23. Remember them? They include love, joy, peace, patience, kindness, goodness, faithfulness, humility, and self-control. When your actions are defined by words like that, then the Spirit quickly opens the lives of others to the Lord through you.

Here are five Christian frustrations very similar to each other. Look them over and think about the answer you might give to each.

One: *"I love my family and they love me very much. But they think I'm a fanatic about Christianity. I'm afraid they are living a lukewarm Christianity. I don't think they know the abundant life they COULD have in Jesus Christ. I guess the real problem lies in our communication. If they knew more about my spiritual life in Christ maybe they would understand it better."*

Two: *"I became a Christian last year and my parents really disapprove of it. They are 'Sunday morning' Christians and have told me I can't make Christianity my whole life. This really hurts but I understand because my half-sister almost joined a religious cult and they're scared for me. I tell them knowing more about the truth will keep me away from such things. There are constant arguments and put-downs. All of us are unhappy."*

Three: *"I'm always having arguments with my parents about religion—they don't seem to understand why I'm so determined. I have just gotten over an ulcer and the only reason I got over it is because I realized I was not alone. I have my Lord and God guiding me."*

Four: *"How can you tell your parents that Christianity is not a religion but an active faith and a true fellowship with the Lord?"*

Five: *"My parents don't understand me and my Christian walk. They think I'm too fanatical so sometimes they try to tell me how I should live and why to do it by the Bible. Well, if I'm so fanatical why do they tell me to live this way? I want to live 100% for Jesus. What do I do when they confront me?"*

Isn't it amazing that parents don't become concerned when children are "fanatical" about things like studies, or work, or materialism, or advancement, or hungering for money, but can be very concerned when their children are "fanatical" about religion? That word *fanatical* actually doesn't mean a whole lot. For many parents, it only means that the young person is more serious about religion than they are—and that can be a very low-level concern! If you're really worried about whether you're fanatical, go back to those "lenses" I talked about earlier. Focus them on the subject of your religious fanaticism. Let them expose you, and your problem, if you have one! See if you're out of kilter. If so, make adjustments. If not, keep at it. Just be sure that you're not acting so smugly self-righteous that no one can stand you, or so viciously Christian that you're ready to destroy for Christ. That kind of tilted lunacy led others, in another age, to start things like the Inquisition. We don't need that kind of wildness, but we do need committed, dedicated, and single-minded followers of Christ. There's nothing wrong with being one. As a matter of fact, it's great. That's not fanaticism—that's elementary discipleship!

What happens if parents are more intensely committed to their faith than they think their children are? What happens if parents are "fanatical"? Listen to this series of statements from teenagers, 16 through 19, of both sexes:

"My mom and I don't go to the same church and she wants me to like what she likes in church and not what I like in church." "The problem is my dad. He's a stubborn Lutheran guy and I'm a regular living-in-Jesus Christian. He wants me to be just like him and wants to live my life for me, but I want to be like Jesus and let Jesus live this life for me! I want to love him, but don't know what that entails. Submitting always or what?"

"My father is a strong believer in God and so am I but he tries to push his way of worshiping on my sister and me. He doesn't realize that times have changed and I have found more meaningful ways to worship. His way is too heavy for me and has no meaning. Maybe it's because he's 50 years old." "My mom told me that I don't know what 'Praise the Lord' means or how to act around someone who is a pastor. That really hurt. It really hurt BAD!!"

Sometimes parents get so hepped up about their church and religion (not necessarily their faith) that they get church and religion and faith all mixed up. One becomes the other. Other parents try to pass on the practices that their parents passed on to them years ago—intact. Example? As one of today's pastors, I'd rather be seen and accepted as an equal and listened to than held in awed respect and ignored. In the past, the pastor was often feared and held in awe. That isn't so today, and I'm glad. The practice of faith changes from generation to generation. Old approaches and attitudes don't always hold up well in the passage of time. Life (including religious life) shifts. I don't believe we're better or worse than the people of the past—just different.

Don't let parents dump old styles of faithfulness on you. Develop your own fresh expressions. But be sure they are just as sincerely expressive of the Christian faith as those styles of the Christ-life you want to set aside. Don't reject something just because your mom or dad suggested it or swallow something hook, line, and sinker for that reason either.

Does having brothers and sisters stimulate "religious" tensions? Do they argue about the faith? Are they likely to struggle in matters of the church? You bet! Here is an example of religious tension that develops between brothers and sisters. An 18-year-old wrote, *"My brother makes me feel like I'm not good enough. Sure I know I'm a sinner and I don't need him to remind me. I cannot understand why it's immoral to have a drink maybe twice a month. But he makes me feel like it's the difference between a Christian and a non-Christian."*

Your brother isn't unique. There are a lot of people in the world that want to make new laws—laws that go beyond anything God has said. That approach is called *legalism.* St. Paul wrote one of his sharpest letters to Christians in Galatia about that very problem. If God has said *no* then the answer is *no.* But wherever God has kept silent, or offers only general direction, you and I function under Christian liberty. That means we cannot be bound by conscience or by the will of God in the matter. We need to be very careful that we don't use that liberty as an excuse for hurting someone or as a way of dulling our witness. Yet we must always recognize and insist upon the difference between a voluntary decision to abstain or restrain ourselves from doing something and a rule that restricts us. In the open spaces between those two extremes, legalism pops up. Avoid it. Witness from the platform of love through those "fruits of the Spirit" that we talked about earlier (Gal. 5:22-23).

My friends, applied Christianity, and life

Many teenagers write to me because they are concerned about the relationship their friends have with Jesus Christ. The nicest thing about these notes is that the writers are reflecting a caring for someone else. They are more than "keepers" of others; in Jesus Christ they have become spiritual brothers and sisters. Look at this sampling of questions.

1) *"Can you turn someone else into a Christian?"*

No, you can't. Only God can do that. But he *wants* to do that, and he may use you as his way of doing it. Take a look at John 3:17. That makes clear his great intent! Be sure you are letting him speak to others through you.

2) *"How does a person go about telling an anti-Christian person about Jesus?"*

The way you do that is by being a witness. That's what Jesus said when he told his disciples in Acts 1:8: ". . . you will be witnesses to me. . . ." That word *witness* describes two things: A witness is someone who has actually experienced something and a witness is always giving a firsthand report of that experience. I cannot witness to the faith of St. Paul—only he can do that. I can tell you about it, I can teach it, but I can't witness to his faith. I can only witness to my own faith. I would answer this question by saying, "You can tell anti-Christian people about Jesus by your words and your deeds. As a matter of fact, I believe you are constantly doing just that." Sometimes your words say that Jesus is important, but your deeds contradict you. A good witness keeps the two in agreement.

3) *"All three of my roommates are non-Christians and sometimes we have a terrible time relating to each other. How should I handle this situation and let it work for the glory of God?"*

That question is from an older teenager already in college. We sometimes have trouble relating to people because of our living habits or the ways we act or our value systems. If we're confident that what we practice is correct and in the best interest of *all*, then the best way to share it with others and relate it to them is by a gentle, kindly, Christ-life. It's not easy. It requires our most sincere effort. But that approach is blessed by God. Don't be a pious pain. Reflect on your circumstances and be guided of God to respond kindly.

4) *"Is it possible for Christians and non-Christians to live together and form relationships on a very personal level when their orientations are often completely at odds?"*

I don't think so. I don't see how. I believe it would result in a compromised Christian position adopted in the interest of unity. Or, if that's not the case, I can only see a life of steady tension, with a piling up of unresolved and unresolvable differences. That's one of the reasons why it's best to seek long-term relationships with practicing Christians. That doesn't mean there will never be any tensions. But practicing Christians know where to go for resolution of their differences. However, I must also tell you that some marriages between Christians and non-Christians have become the best evangelism programs the church has ever had. It's tough facing the problems at first, and may not finally work out, yet when it does, it's wonderful!

5) *"What does a Christian tell a non-Christian when asked what she does for excitement? They'd never understand."*

I laughed at that. They really wouldn't fully understand, would they? But that's no answer. How about this: For one thing, she could say that life itself is very exciting for a Christian. It is! She can tell of the fun it is to be full of joy in God's promise. She can say that everything that builds and blesses was conceived by God and given to us for making our lives better. She can say that, but finally she must just live her life openly and pray that God will persuade others of the joy that she has found. Do let people know about the fun you're having living as a Christian. One way to do that is by smiling a lot. If the life in Christ is such a grim burden that you can never look pleased or pleasant, then I wonder if you have picked up the wrong load. He tells us that his yoke is easy and his load is light (Matt. 11:30).

Whenever you have a problem in your relationship with God, you don't really have much of a problem. The Lord will deal with you, he will touch you in a marvelous way —sometimes through his Word, sometimes through the power of prayer. Take your needs to him. He will respond. Search his Word for specific direction. It's amazing how he has anticipated many of our concerns and provided just the direction that will get us through. Remember that his clearest directions are always those which take us by his grace and mercy to the Savior.

Many of the "religious" questions and concerns that people have, teenagers included, don't have much to do with God or his Word. Somehow or other we get churchy rules and human practices and family customs all mixed up with the plan of salvation which God has given. If you're involved in a "religious" discussion, be sure that the discussion is genuinely religious. Otherwise you are just arguing about human odds and ends which have no final answer.

Many of us have a love-hate relationship to the church. We respect, honor, and like it, yet, at the same time, we are upset about the way it acts and some of the things it has done in the past. We are surprised to discover that the greatest problem with the church is that there are sinners in it. As a matter of fact, that's *all* there is in the church! Just sinners—like us. But, by the grace of God, we know that we are forgiven sinners. In the meanwhile, we fail to live up to our Christian potential! It's OK to see the church as flawed and sometimes wrong and insensitive and sometimes less than God wants. All that is very true. But that's not all the truth there is. Be sure you look closely at the many extremely dedicated and loving Christians who also sit in those pews and who rise above their sinful nature. Look with care toward the many remarkably fine pastors who, by God's grace, overcome the inadequacies in their own struggle of faith and offer powerful Christian witness. Look hungrily for teachers who pass on the faith with a joy and ability that's really unusual and you will have your yearnings satisfied. Look for all those things. You will find them!

Then make a list. List all the church's flaws. But don't stop with just listing. Ask yourself, "How can I help

change these faults?" Begin with that kind of attitude in your teenage years and continue, through the rest of your life, to seek ways to help. Help change the church for the better so that there might be an increasingly joyful and positive atmosphere in which you can live out your life. Help change the church for others who, through what you do, will hear the clear voice of the Savior speaking in the congregation. Help the changing process for your children and for others who will need to see the church function at its best. Help straighten it all out. Then, when you pass it on to the next generation, it will be better for having been touched by you.

Do something good for your pastor—talk to him. Talk to him about ways in which you can become more active and involved in the ministry of the people of God at the place which is your church home. Pray for him. Love him. Encourage him. Work with him. Tell him about the good things he has done. He will be blessed by you. You will be blessed in him. Together you will be a great power for good, and for the glorifying of God, in the place where you live. You'll never believe how well you can get along in God's church until you try. And once you try, you'll never want to exchange it for anything.

EIGHT

Getting Along in Our Troubled World

I deeply admire the young people of today and their accomplishments in the face of so many testings. Some days I wonder what I would be like if I were growing up now. Without idealizing or dramatizing the past (I know nothing is ever as good or as bad as one's memory sketches), life then was very simple in comparison to today, and my moral testings were nowhere near as intense as those today's teenagers face. Let me explain.

I never saw a pornographic movie as a teenager. I was never even tempted to see one. Why? There weren't any. Or, if there were pornographic movies, they were shown so secretly that none of the kids I grew up with knew anything about them. Drugs were things you bought at the drugstore for a headache or a bad cold. "Smoking weed" meant puffing away on a cigarette.

Moral standards were significantly different then too. Maybe we were more hypocritical in our actions and maybe we hid more from the reality of life, but moral expectations were very different. Sexual experimentation, living together before marriage, nude floor shows, and any of a hundred different assaults on the moral levels of today's kids were not tolerated, let alone condoned. If a girl became pregnant before marriage, she was described as someone who "got in trouble." While there was still immorality enough for anyone, the tone and texture of that immorality was much more subtle and subdued than it is today. It just wasn't the same.

I think many of today's teenagers face more spiritual testings before noon than I dealt with during all my teenage years. I pray intensely for the young men and women who have to struggle so much harder to stand strong in the Lord in our time. In addition, I'm very ashamed that I must take my share of the blame for the atmosphere of degeneration in which they must grow up. As an adult, I allow it to exist, and I'm sorry.

Yet, let me witness to you of the mighty army of today's young people who are spiritually stable and incredibly strong in their convictions. They share with me their testings and their daily problems. In our society, immorality is tolerated, accepted, expected, and, in some places, even encouraged and admired. But a lot of Christian young men and women disappoint those who have that kind of view.

Teenagers! Take a strong stand on morality. Put the blame where it belongs. You aren't the ones who publish sexually explicit material. You don't produce and then screen lurid movies. You don't write the laws that encourage drug abuse, alcoholism, prostitution, and an incredibly wide span of abusively immoral activity. That "honor" belongs to those of us who are much older. And the honor for tolerating that kind of trash belongs to the older ones as well. I don't see a lot of people past their 40s publicly taking firm moral stands in the face of all the filth with which we're surrounded. It looks to me that those who are young today will have to lead the way in destroying what so many of us have allowed to develop. And, thanks be to God, I see evidence of that determination wherever I go. Let those of you who are pushing toward cleanliness press on. Clean up the 20th century Sodom and Gomorrahs! God knows there are enough of them. You need not tolerate an atmosphere of moral filth. Get your life together and commit yourself to lifelong combat *for* the Lord and *against* the works of Satan.

In Chapter 6 I shared some of the concerns teenagers have about their sexual feelings and the pressures our world today places on them. In this last chapter I want to focus on some additional areas of moral tension which teens ask about. To set the stage for this discussion, let's begin by talking about the word *use*.

When people use people

In my estimation, that word *use* is the king of all obscenities in our language. Any of the well-known four-letter expressions are only examples of what it means to use someone. *How* you use other people is not as important as *that* you use them.

When you use people, you turn them into "things." You depersonalize them. As a matter of fact, you *must* depersonalize people before you use them. Make a person a rock, a piece of dirty paper, a clump of weeds—who cares? In depersonalizing, you set the stage for using.

The mind-set of turning people into things and using them triggers such frightening abuses as rape, robbery, sexual manipulation, seduction, addiction, alcoholism, homosexuality, lesbianism, battering, muggings, murders, thefts, degeneracy, and everything else that is immoral and hurts people. Before anything like that happens, someone becomes a "thing." Sometimes that "thing" is you! Think about that, and before you move much further in life, make a threefold commitment to yourself. Say:

1) I won't treat myself as a "thing."
2) I won't let anyone else treat me as a "thing."
3) I won't treat anyone else as a "thing."

Does that sound simple? Review that list. Think about each commitment. Was there ever a time when you were the victim someone turned into a "thing"? Have you ever "used" someone for your pleasure? Were you ever manipulated by others for their desires? Think about it. If you haven't already done so, confess whatever sins surface in your memory and ask God to forgive you. Then ask him for strength to resist either using others or letting yourself be used. With his forgiveness and the assurance that he will answer your prayer, you are on your way toward a new attitude.

Problems with parents: alcohol and child abuse

I'll let the kids tell you about it. *"How can I, as a girl, tell my father I want him to stop drinking without hav-*

ing my father say to me he has the feeling that I am defying him?" "How do you talk to an alcoholic parent?" "My father drinks too much and sometimes makes fun of the fact that I am a Christian." "My father and mother are separated. My dad is an alcoholic. I don't know how to talk or relate to him very well."

More: "My dad drinks beer all the time and we can't get him to quit. When he drinks no one can talk to him because he won't listen." "My parents are OK when they haven't been drinking (and that's not that often.)" "How do you deal with parents who have an alcoholic problem?" "My father embarrasses my friends. Sometimes he drinks and then really embarrasses me and my friends."

And more: "I have a problem with a father who is divorced and remarried—he is unhappy. But he is an alcoholic, he is very paranoid and thinks the world's out to get him. What to do?" "I told my dad he was an alcoholic and he got mad." "My mother drinks. She has to drink on weekends. And the problem is she can't have just one. She has to have two, three, and then four. My dad and I think she's hooked. She'll think up excuses to drink during the week, too, but again she won't stop. Help me."

Those statements were written by kids between the ages of 12 and 17. All do not deal with full-blown alcoholism, but all of them speak of problems that look like alcoholism. Whenever you're facing an alcoholic parent, you need to talk with someone. Among the "someones" with whom you can talk are pastors, school counselors, good friends, teachers, or caring relatives. At the very least, you'll get to temporarily unload that burden of anguish which living with an alcoholic brings.

As a further and very important step, get in touch with Alcoholics Anonymous. You can generally find this organization in your phone book. If your phone book doesn't have such a group listed, call a local hospital or the county mental health association. Try the police station. If you are nervous and reluctant, make the call anonymously. Talk to someone there. Most people who are connected with Alcoholics Anonymous have been alcoholics themselves. They know your pain. They will talk to you.

Associated with many Alcoholics Anonymous organizations is another group called Alateen. It helps teenagers who have to live with the problems of alcoholism. There is also a group called Alanon that helps families. And there are others! Help is to be had and you're a foolish person if you don't go get it.

But be prepared to tell the truth. Share the specifics and they will let you know whether you are dealing with a drinking problem or whether you have an exaggerated and warped sense of what's right and wrong. Make sure you recognize the difference. Calling someone an alcoholic when they aren't doesn't help. But leading someone to see that he is an alcoholic, when such is the case, is a very caring and important process. You need to talk with someone about the particular set of circumstances in which you find yourself, and there are people around you who dearly want to help. You need not confront this problem alone. Get the help you need. You're old enough now to take that step on your own. If it's any comfort, there are an awful lot of Christian young people just like you who are working with the same concern.

Alcoholism isn't the only problem with parents. There are in this world some very sick mothers and fathers who use excessive physical force to punish or correct little children—or do so just to get some sort of twisted delight. When the person beaten is an infant, we talk about "battered babies." *This activity is against the law.* Not only is it offensive before God, but it is an activity the courts of our land find offensive as well. It is estimated that about three percent of all children are battered.

That battering of children does not stop when the children grow up. It often continues into the teens. Here are a few of the comments I have received: *"My parents treat me like a moron, and whenever I try to talk to them they turn the conversation into a one-sided lecture and if I act bored my father hits me." "I can't openly discuss my views with my parents. They dominate the conversation. Their punishment is physical." "My conflict is with my dad—he's violent and if I don't share his values and views, he gets very 'upset.'" "My mom really has a problem. She is always yelling at me and hitting me no matter what I do."*

Adults who batter children of any age really want to be helped. Some don't know how to get it—or don't have the courage to take the first step. *Get help for them.*

Many people who batter others were battered themselves when they were children. That's you—if you are now being battered. The pattern has to be broken. The terrifying sequence has to be stopped. *Get help not only for your parents, but for yourself.*

Where do you go? Go back to that list of people who can help with alcoholic parent problems. In an emergency, call the police. When you share with others, be truthful. Hold nothing back. You're not out for vengeance. Battering parents need help. Get it for them.

I don't think I have to tell you that there is a lot of difference between spanking and battering. If you're not sure which is which, call a trusted individual anonymously and describe what has happened to you. Let them help decide your problem. Ask them if they think you need help and listen to their advice.

Not only are three percent of American children battered, but another study indicates that three percent of young people—usually girls—are sexually abused by a member of their immediate family: a father, a brother, a grandfather, an uncle, or a close friend. Get help for them too. Sexually abusing a child is immoral and illegal. Often a sexually abused young girl keeps quiet about what has happened, feeling ashamed or somehow responsible. *Don't* keep quiet. Go to those same helping people already mentioned. Tell them your problem. Describe what has happened. Let them help you.

I first began talking about this kind of sexual abuse before large gatherings a couple of years ago. After one of my first presentations, a young lady came to me. She wanted to talk. She said she felt guilty and dirty and unforgiven and sinful. I told her none of that was true. She was the victim. She was not guilty of her father's sin. I assured her, and her father, of God's forgiveness in Christ —that whoever confesses and seeks forgiveness receives it. She made me promise that whenever I spoke before a large group, I would do my best to make this concern a part of my presentation. I have, and I have yet to make these comments before a large group without at least one person thanking me. Here's a typical letter:

"Your openness about problems teens face was great. It took me a long time before I confided with anyone about the abnormal relations my father had with me. I never told anyone until right before my marriage. I felt

I had to tell my future husband. My father had been sexually abusing me, and it took me a long time before I could even say that. I have no guilt about what happened and I have shared my past with a lot of teens. Somehow their knowing I made it makes them feel like they, too, can get through a lot. I wish when I was a teen someone would have been as candid as you. I would have confided in someone. Please keep talking that candidly. The young people really need to hear you."

Don't carry around a guilt that is not yours. Don't be shamed into secrecy about something for which you're not responsible. Get help for everyone concerned—including yourself. Encourage others to speak up too. Exposing this sin is the best way to control it!

Problems with yourself: smoking, booze, and drugs

The notes I just shared dealt with problems of parents with which kids had to live. The notes in this section are about the kids themselves. They write to me about their personal struggles with the effects of smoking, booze, and drugs.

Smoking means cigarette smoking. Teenage concerns sound like this: *"The main problem is my mom and I fight all the time, and also another problem is I smoke. My mom and dad fuss about it. They smoke, so do you think it's fair for them to hassle me? I guess I should quit—I'm trying."*

It's almost impossible to live in our society and not realize that smoking cigarettes is a form of slow death. But it takes some people a long time to see that—I know it did me! When I finally quit smoking and started experiencing things the way they'd always been (my sense of taste and smell had been so dulled I didn't realize what I was missing), I could have kicked myself for all I had missed. I don't doubt for a moment that I was addicted to nicotine. But I can testify that it's possible to quit after more than 30 years of smoking. I know. I did it.

One of the most powerful supports in stopping smoking is prayer. If you are trying to quit smoking, pray for yourself. If someone you care about is trying to quit, pray for him or her, and urge that person to pray. Make a personal request in love. I know of a number of fathers and mothers who quit smoking because their children asked them. Don't tell a parent or friend how bad it smells; ask them to quit because you love them and want them to be around for some very important moments coming in your life and in their own. Help them stop using themselves.

If you want to stop smoking my best advice is simple: Stop. Don't get suckered in with the argument that begins, "I wish I could quit." That's baloney and you know it. Stop using yourself. You have no more right to destroy yourself than anyone else would have to destroy you. If you don't understand that smoking *does* affect your body, then your problem is that you are living under a rock. Don't kid yourself—it can kill you.

You don't look great while smoking. You don't smell great while smoking. And, before long, you won't sound great while smoking. My personal witness to you is that there isn't enough smoking pleasure in the world to pay for the years of other joys I lost. And there's nothing that will get me going again. Why wait till you're my age (if you make it) to say that? Quit now.

Smoking is a drug—but it's not the only one. I've noticed that the days young people packed lecture halls when the use of drugs was being discussed are over. There are as many people involved with drugs now as before, but group discussions have dwindled. That doesn't mean interest has waned. Kids tell me that *group* interest has slowed down, but the individual notes and letters from kids keep coming!

Why the inconsistency? I think teenagers steer clear of drug discussion groups because those groups usually spend their time focusing on the "facts" of drugs. Most kids already know the facts. What they don't know is how those facts fit into their lives. They need someone to give them the moral texture for the discussion of drugs. Let me give you a flavoring of the questions and comments I receive on the subject of drugs (and drinking and smoking).

"My parents hassle me about drugs and late hours." *"I'm my own problem. I'm mixed up and confused. I don't want to drink, but the pressure from my friends is so intense that I end up doing it. No matter how hard I try to ignore what they say, I can't."* *"What can we do for friends that have tried suicide and are falling into the*

drug scene?" "I'm a frequent user of marijuana (at least twice a week). It is something that I enjoy; however it does not interfere with my stewardship because I don't invest more than $1 per week and it does not take time away from my studies, my family, or from God."

"My problem is that I've just found out that two of my best friends (since kindergarten) smoke pot and drink. We've talked about it before and they know how I feel about it; I thought they felt the same. What can I do?" "My younger brother takes drugs. I don't. My parents are almost in shock about the situation and I'm worried. We feel like we can't talk to him—he never listened before and we're afraid he won't listen now—just turn us off. What do we do?" "The thing disturbing my life right now is conflict with my parents because of skipping school and drugs."

"I'm confused about drinking and smoking weed. I don't do it excessively, and I only drink when I'm thirsty. Is it a sin to do it?" "My mother was very upset when I came home at 2:01 after a very meaningful youth fellowship meeting, but was not upset when I came home at 12 drunk." "My problem is using drugs and drinking and smoking."

Rather than dealing with each of the specific concerns one by one, I want to share a series of reactions to the entire category of concerns. I hope my reactions will stimulate you to think through the same problems.

1) Anything that significantly dulls or artificially impairs your attitudes or life-style is not good. And anything that can be shown to seriously affect your body or has potential for damaging the children you will have someday is not good. Have nothing to do with anything like that. You don't even need to argue about it. Just don't!

2) Don't act as if intelligent people are still trying to decide whether drugs can seriously affect you or not. We aren't waiting for a scientific conclusion on the subject. That conclusion has already been offered. Drugs do those things I mentioned above. Some drugs affect you more quickly and with greater intensity than others. No drug leaves you unscathed, and don't kid yourself that it does.

3) People who warn others about drugs and who try to destroy the drug business are not old-fashioned med-

dlers. They are smart folks, caring individuals, dear friends. Listen to them.

4) "There is none so deaf as he who will not hear." So unplug your ears.

5) Don't use yourself. Don't use others. Don't let others use you. That's what drugs and drinking and smoking are all about. They are ways to practice using.

If you don't believe Item 2 above, then reread Item 4. The radical and long-term effects of all drugs (marijuana included) are a proven fact. There is a destructive genetic effect that is passed on to your children through your use of drugs. If you realize all I have said is true, and you still continue to use drugs, then you are badly bent. You are emotionally and intellectually out of kilter, and desperately distorted. Seek counsel—you need some help. Ask for it. You can get it. Don't whimper in the corner and complain that things are happening to you when you are the one starting the action. *Don't use yourself.*

Those last paragraphs are the least "preachy" and most straightforward words I can write. I've written them to many young people and said them just as clearly before audiences. I don't know how to speak more plainly. Those words are true—don't let anyone (yourself included) tell you any different.

There are many other things that I could report to you about the "real" world in which we live. But you know about that world, don't you? What I have written is a composite of the things my teenage friends (like you) tell me about or ask me about or which surface in our discussions. More than that, it's a report on how God in his goodness responds to our many concerns and forgives our many mistakes.

Whenever you feel uncomfortable about something you're doing, that's a pretty good indication you should back off. Pause. Ask others about it. Search the Scriptures for God's word of guidance and direction for you. You'll find it. He has no hidden messages. You might miss one or two "good" things in the world by following that advice. *You might.* But you'll most assuredly miss many grievous experiences and painful moments. And you'll also be walking the way of the abundant life!

Getting along as a Christian doesn't mean that you have

to compromise with anyone—or anything. It doesn't mean you have to pass the good times and swallow the bitter pills of loneliness. Not at all. Getting along as a Christian teenager means that you walk the way Jesus walked through his teenage years when he, under the Spirit's guidance, "grew both in body and wisdom, gaining favor with God and men" (Luke 2:52). I hope that you, too, will have that same "increasing" experience our Lord Jesus had. Ask for his guiding hand throughout all your life. Walking through the teenage years, then on into all the remaining years, with him is the greatest way I know for getting along.